Frances Ridley Havergal

⊰⊱ HYMNWRITER ⊰⊱

FRANCES RIDLEY HAVERGAL

❧ HYMNWRITER ❧

Esther E. Enock

AMBASSADOR
Belfast • Greenville

Frances Ridley Havergal ~ Hymnwriter

ISBN   1   898787   68   9

Published by

AMBASSADOR PRODUCTIONS, LTD.
Providence House
16 Hillview Avenue,
Belfast, BT5 6JR

Emerald House
1 Chick Springs Road, Suite 206
Greenville, South Carolina, 29609

Printed in Northern Ireland

List of Contents

Take my life, and let it be
Consecrated, Lord, to Thee;
Take my moments and my days,
Let them flow in ceaseless praise.

Take my hands, and let them move
At the impulse of Thy love;
Take my feet, and let them be
Swift and beautiful for Thee.

Take my voice, and let me sing
Always, only for my King;
Take my lips, and let them be
Filled with messages from Thee.

Take my silver and my gold,
Not a mite would I withhold:
Take my intellect, and use
Every power as Thou shalt choose.

Take my will, and make it Thine;
It shall be no longer mine:
Take my heart, it is Thine own;
It shall be Thy royal throne.

Take my love; my Lord, I pour
At Thy feet its treasure-store:
Take myself, and I will be
Ever, only, all for Thee.

CHAPTER ONE

Little Quicksilver

 "Fanny dear, pray to God to prepare you for all He is preparing for you," said the dying mother to her little girl in pleading, solemn tones.

Frances Ridley Havergal was about eleven years of age when these words were spoken to her, but she would not believe that her beloved mother was dying. As she says in her autobiography, she shut her eyes in a very hardened way to those who tried to prepare her for it. Mrs Havergal was quite aware of this, and strove to lead her child to trust and love the Saviour that she might have comfort when the heavy blow should fall.

"You are my youngest little girl, and I feel more anxious about you than the rest. I do pray for the Holy Spirit to lead and guide you. And remember, nothing but the precious blood of Christ cam make you clean and lovely in God's sight."

"Oh, mamma, I'm sure you will get well again," and not even the mother's solemnly glad affirmation that she would soon see her Saviour face to face could penetrate those wilfully closed little ears.

When the end had really come, the child, highly strung and highly imaginative, hoped, until almost the very day of the funeral that her mother was only in a trance. She had heard of people supposed to be dead who had recovered, and so, again and again she tiptoed into that room and stook looking upon the lovely face, half expecting the eyes to unclose and smile at her.

Poor child! they did not do so, and it was a grief-stricken little Frances who, on that sad day, peeped through a tiny space between blind and window to watch the funeral procession pass through the Rectory gates into the church.

Mrs Havergal died on 5th July, 1848, and little Frances wrote verses suitable for one who had entered Heaven, which show how clear was her head-knowledge of the truth; but, alas, her heart was as yet unreached.

Her grief over her mother's death was very great, but not always evident. Her lively disposition enabled her to put it away and engage for the moment, intensely, on whatever she was doing. These versatile moods were often misunder-stood. A gay laugh, a sudden rush upstairs and downstairs, made the others think little Frances had not many sad thoughts. Little did they realise in those days how heavy the child's heart often was only a moment before the lively little outburst.

Frances ridley Havergal, the subject of this story, known to thousands by her writings as FRH, was born 14th December, 1836. She was the youngest of a family of six - and the beloved pet of all.

FRH was always very proud of her middle name "Ridley". It was the name of her godfather, Rev WH Ridley, Rector of Hambleden, who was descended from Bishop Ridley. It is safe to say that this quick and imaginative child would often picture to herself the morning when the noble martyr stood at his stake "on the north side of the town (Oxford), in the ditch over against Baliol College. She would see Ridley in his black furred gown, Latimer just behind, approaching the spot - she would hear Ridley's voice saying to Latimer: "Be of good cheer, brother, for God will either assauge the fury of the flame, or else strengthen us to abide it." Then came the tying to the stake, and the kindling of the faggots - and now it is Latimer who says: "Be of good comfort, brother Ridley, and play the man; we shall this day light such a candle by God's grace in England, as I trust shall never be put out." The lighting of the candle was agony to him, but still we see it. *It has never been put out*.

And so the name "Ridley" was to FRH, as she says in a pretty poetic outburst, "a diamond clasp." What part that name played in her powers of endurance we cannot say exactly, but it could not fail to influence her.

Her father named and delighted to call her "Little Quicksilver," a name quite indicative of her disposition in childhood's years. She was bright, quick, and clever far beyond her age, and there was need to restrain the eagerness with which she would have advanced.

Her sister, Miriam, was her first teacher, and found her to be a charming little pupil. She could speak distinctly at two years old, and at three was able to read easy books. Very often she was hidden away under the table with some absorbing story. At four years she was able to read the Bible and any ordinary book, also to write in roundhand.

She was born at Astley Rectory, where her father was Rector for twenty years. He left there when Frances was about six years old for a temporary home at Henwick House, Hallow. Three years later, 1845, the family moved to St Nicholas Rectory, Worcester, where Frances was deprived of her beloved country surroundings. She missed them very much, but there was some compensation in the fact that she had a little room all to herself. From its window the expanse of sky and clouds made up in some degree for the trees and grass she had enjoyed before.

She always longed to climb the great white clouds - they looked as if they were firm enough to rest upon - until she learned that, like all other clouds, they were but mist and rain. In her spiritual conflict before conversion, and in her efforts to obtain peace, she was often cloud-climbing in this way, inevitably proving the uselessness of anything and everything except the Blood of Jesus Christ, which cleanses from all sin, to give rest and security.

This is what I mean by her cloud-climbing. She would go to bed and determine to think about God, but her thoughts, as she said, did not flow heavenward, naturally, any more than water flows upward; or she would try to force them into a definite channel by a half whisper telling herself: How good it was of God to send Jesus to die; and it all generally ended in her crying bitterly because she knew that she did not believe that wonderful goodness for herself. Other nights she would lie awake praying for faith, and she also spent much time reading her Bible. But all this did not save her, and her substantial-looking clouds faded away.

Up to the age of six years, she said, she had not any thoughts or ideas on religion, but after that time she began to long (to use her own words) "to be a Christian." And yet, as we have seen, how readily she would trust those yearnings aside, resisting even that dear, dying mother, who, even when Frances was only four had tenderly taught her about the Lord Jesus. It shows how eagerly Satan tries to hinder us from finding the Saviour.

But during all her strivings after peace, and during the days when she did not trouble at all, little Frances always knew the sinfulness of her heart. Never was she tempted, as some people are, to say she was "as good as others;" she always knew herself as a great and helpless sinner, and that even when she was between eight and fourteen years old. It is a good thing to know that great truth, whatever the age. And so these five years passed away in changeful feelings and hopes and fears. She read her Bible frequently, for she was determined to find that Eternal Life of which it spoke. Every day for an hour this hungry child read it, especially the New Testament; but her diligence met with no reward at that time.

When she was about 13, in 1850, she went to Belmont, near Campden Hill, a Boarding School where there were more than a hundred girls.

The Principal, Mrs Teed, a godly, loving woman, whose heart yearned to lead her girls to the Saviour, was concluding her long course of school work, and prayed that this last year should see the conversion of many, and that none should leave her house unimpressed.

Her desire was abundantly granted. Among the converts were some of Frances' dearest friends. The first was "Mary". Mary was one of the number of girls who were known as Christians by their conversation and behaviour, and by the peace and joy which shone in their faces. To Mary, after some time, Frances opened her heart, and Mary did her best to lead her longing schoolfellow into the light. Many were the talks they had.

Later, Elizabeth, another friend, was saved, and she, too, did what she could for FRH, but no relief came. The poor child, hearing one and another speaking in terms of confidence and gladness, felt her heart sink lower than ever, so unattainable did such a state of soul seem to her.

November passed, and earnestness among the girls increased. Joy and peace in believing was written on many faces; pupils spoke reverently and joyously of the treasure of salvation, of the knowledge of sins forgiven. Poor Frances wept and prayed every night. On Sunday, 8th December, Diana was converted. Diana was loved by all; she was especially beloved by FRH, and no one thought Diana was anything but converted long before, so sweet and so consistently good and gentle was she. Diana, before this second birthday of hers, had kept herself rather aloof for some days, and Frances had noticed some slight depression on her, and wondered what had caused it.

But on this Sunday, December 8th, when Frances took her seat opposite Diana at tea time, that depression had vanished entirely. There was, instead, a wonderful radiance on Diana's face - a wonderful gladness in her voice. FRH looked on her with awe. What could have come to Diana?

Diana did not keep her friend waiting long. Directly tea was over, she came to her, and sitting at her side, told how the blessing had come to her at last. She knew she was forgiven for Jesus' sake. And now He was her Saviour, far above all she had dared to hope. Then she begged Frances to come to Him - "Come, and He will receive you."

How Frances longed to come! How she yearned for that joy unspeakable which her friend had. But the days passed on, and Frances found herself once more at home, and still unsaved. A weary time of seeking followed, with now and then a bright gleam to lead her on, and to stay her despair.

It was not till two months later, February, 1851, that she really trusted her soul to the Lord Jesus. She was visiting at Oakhampton, the home of her sister Miriam, Mrs Henry Crane. Miss Cooke, who afterwards married Frances' father, was also on a visit. She was the means of helping Frances to the point of trusting alone in Christ Jesus.

They had many talks, and one day she asked Frances point blank why she could not trust the Saviour at once. Could she not commit her soul to Him? Was not His promise enough?

Breathlessly, Frances replied: "I could trust Him, surely!" and she flew upstairs filled with hope.

In her room, though still with a slight admixture of fear, she did trust Jesus - she did commit her soul to Him, believing He was able *to keep it* against that day. She knew that she was saved! Oh, joy - peace!

From then onward her real happiness lay in pleasing and serving Him. It had been a long and weary struggle, but when she was older she felt that she would know, someday, the meaning of those long years of restlessness and dissatisfaction which were her portion in early childhood, when every one thought her carefree and happy.

Lord, speak to me, that I may speak
In living echoes of Thy tone;
As Thou hast sought, so let me seek
Thy erring children lost and lone.

O lead me, Lord, that I may lead
The wandering and the wavering feet;
O feed me, Lord, that I may feed
Thy hungering ones with manna sweet.

O strengthen me, that, while I stand
Firm on the Rock, and strong in Thee,
I may stretch out a loving hand
To wrestlers with the troubled sea.

O teach me, Lord, that I may teach
The precious things Thou dost impart;
And wing my words, that they may reach
The hidden depths of many a heart.

O give Thine own sweet rest to me,
That I may speak with soothing power
A word in season, as from Thee,
To weary ones in needful hour.

O fill me with Thy fulness, Lord,
Until my very heart o'erflow
In kindling thought and glowing word,
Thy love to tell, Thy praise to show.

O use me, Lord, use even me,
Just as Thou wilt, and when, and where,
Until Thy blessed face I see,
Thy rest, Thy joy, Thy glory share.

CHAPTER TWO

Growing Up and Growing in Grace

In July of that same year (1851) the Rev WH Havergal married Miss Caroline Ann Cooke, an event which proved most happy for all, her loving care of her husband evidently prolonged his life.

In August, Frances again went to school at Powick House, near Worcester, but in less than four months she was obliged to relinquish her studies and return home on account of erysipelas in her head and face. A long period of inaction followed, which was very trying to one of such an active disposition as "little Quicksilver."

She wrote to her friend, Elizabeth Clay, from Colwyn Bay, August, 1852, where she was staying with her parents. In this letter she expresses regret at the impatience she felt at hearing the dreadful news that she was not to go to school again till after Christmas - perhaps not at all! Her disappointment was great, for she loved learning.

From November, 1852, to December, 1853, a period of thirteen months, Frances was in Germany with her parents. Rev WH Havergal had incipient cataract, and went to Gräfrath, to consult Dr de Leuw, the great oculist. To Frances' great delight she was allowed to go to school in Dusseldorf, named Louisenchule, after the Queen of Prussia. It was a public school, and had one hundred and ten scholars. The letters from FRH from this place are pictures of her eager sensitive mind - so keen on study, so regretful that at times earthly learning tempted her to forget to grow in the knowledge of her Lord and Saviour.

The school was under the supervision of Pastor Kraft, a good man, and the Mistress was Fraulein Quincke. Mr Havergal felt he might safely leave his sixteen-year-old daughter there, whilst he and his wife travelled about. Frances was delighted at the decision, for she had already spent a term there, and had obtained an excellent testimony from the examiners. Among the hundred and ten girls she found not one who cared for religion, and this fact put her on her mettle, so to speak. She felt she must display the Royal Banner bravely. She simply *must* walk worthy of her calling, and work to win souls for Him. She became more earnest and watchful lest by some thoughtless word, or deed, she should shame Him before her schoolfellows.

Of course there was persecution in a small way of the *"Englanderin,"* but Frances did not mind. She considered that it compelled her to take a higher stand than ever she had previously taken.

The result among her schoolfellows seemed to be nil, but who can tell? She owns that some were disarmed - left off persecuting, and became affectionate. Such a testimony as FRH bore in the Louisenschule could not fail to bear fruit. "Them that honour Me. I will honour."

Perhaps now she sees some results in that Land whither she has gone.

Between term FRH had a month's holiday in Königswinter with her parents. She speaks of Münster, the capital, where she and her father paid a visit to the Cathedral, whilst Mrs Havergal rested at the hotel. The bells were ringing, and inside, the soft faint light was entrancing. The sound of the bells here was like sweet chanting by a choir. There were solitary worshippers with book and tapers before their favourite images or crosses. She could well understand how the quite, peaceful feeling around might be mistaken for personal devotion and spirituality - whereas it was just the senses and feelings entrapped by outward things. Then she speaks of seeing a confirmation next morning, and how, at the sound of a little bell the congregation knelt as the host was elevated. "All well suited as a religion for the natural heart," was her shrewd comment.

Back at school again, she plunged into her beloved studies, and again fearful at times lest the eager desire for, and pursuit of, earthly knowledge should make her forgetful and carless of heavenly things. I do not think this happened, though she was "numero one" in the Louisenschule.

She left school "for ever" In September, 1853, and bemoans the fact in a letter to her life-long friend, Elizabeth Clay. She declared that it bought a suffocating feeling to realise that school days were over, and life's responsibilities increased tenfold.

But the family did not return to England. They spent some time at Obercassel on the Rhine, within view of the Drachenfels. Mr Havergal's eyes were still troubling him, and during the completion of the cure FRH was with Pastor Schulze-Berge and his wife, where she was very happy studying German composition, literature, and history. She won high praise from Pastor Schulze-Berge, and after her death he wrote to her sister, MJG Havergal, author of "Memorials of FRH," a letter such as would rejoice that sister's heart. He speaks of the stamp of nobility upon her - the deep reverence she had for the Lord Jesus Christ, and said he had seldom been so touched by any news as that of her early Home-call. This letter, which was written twenty-six years after her residence in his house, is evidence that the fragrance of her character lingered there still. Frances, at seventeen years of age, had impressed the whole household with her sanctity and sincerity.

CHAPTER THREE

Some Quiet Years

 In her earlier letters, Frances Ridley Havergal affords us a glimpse of the adventurous spirit she possessed.

It was in 1852, her sixteenth year, that she wrote of a visit to Llandudno, with her sister Ellen and her brother Frank. The copper mines in Orme's Head attracted her, and she was impatient to be underground. Consequently when the men had left work, these three packed themselves one evening into a little truck, like the trucks on Haytor, Dartmoor, and were pushed half a mile into the tunnel. Daylight became a mere star behind them; then they got out and followed their friendly pusher into curious caves of crystals and copper ore, and she feasted her eyes with the strange surroundings. Thence after a brief exploration, they returned again to the outer air.

She says they had many walks, but she preferred exploring alone, and on these solitary excursions she got into very breakneck places. She avers she was almost too venturesome, but adds her foot had not slipped once. It would seem she was far more anxious about spiritual than material slipping, and she confessed to many slips in the former way; at least they appeared slips to her sensitive conscience. Perhaps many of us would not notice such slips in our spiritual walk.

She speaks, too, of the wild places she would get into, and then, out would come her little Testament, and she would read and pray - secure that in that inaccessible spot she would be undisturbed.

Next, we hear that she is upset because she bathed too much. She would, of course. The sparkling water, the exhilarating movement of swimming, and the delight of floating, would tempt her to remain in the water too long.

Well, FRH was extremely sorry to find her sea bathing put a stop to, for she liked mounting the waves as much as she enjoyed riding the "wicked little pony" the family possessed.

She knew how to be grave as well as gay, for she speaks of a boy who is going back to school, wondering if he will be able to stand firm there. She says it is more difficult to be prayerful at school than anywhere. At Powick School, Worcester, which she attended after leaving Miss Teed's Belmont, she began prayerfully, but gradually lost, she says.

Miss Elizabeth Clay, to whom this girlish, interesting letter is written, has evidently been having bright spiritual experiences, as FRH says she wishes that some fairy slippers would transport EC to her side on the high place in which she sits above the waves.

In 1854 she was at Tenby, where she rode *ad libitum* with a Powick schoolgirl friend. The church there, she tells EC, is large, but the pews "excerably uncomfortable." The curate who preached spoke with a heart full of love to his Saviour, and was anxious that God's love should be known and believed by every one - the love that God hath to us, in that He sent His Son to die for our sins.

In 1854 still, from St Nicholas Rectory, we find her successful in winning prizes for poetical enigmas in a competition. She won six books - kept one, and sold five for missionary work.

In 1855 Mr Havergal was at Gräfrath again, for treatment for his eyes. I do not know if they stayed at the same hotel in which they were on the occasion of the first visit. Of the master of that hotel, Miss Havergal says, "he was extremely fond of cats and dogs." She used to smile as she listened to the patter of fifty-two little feet going upstairs with him every night. (In this case fifty-two feet means thirteen four-footed animals.)

Frances Ridley Havergal was not with her parents during this second visit, but at her sister Miriam's at Oakhampton. She returned home to receive the travellers, however, and before they arrived she had done a great deal in the way of decoration. She had erected an arch over the hall door with flowers and greenery. The study door had her father's crest in flowers, and over the dining room door was displayed a banner with "Welcome Home" done in rosebuds and leaves. Her father was able to see it all, and that was the crowning joy.

Her delight that her father would be in the reading desk once more, after nearly four years, was expressed in this and many other gracious acts.

In 1857, from St Nicholas Rectory, she writes to her sister, describing Whitsuntide proceedings.

Mr James, their curate, was "very cool and amusing." His sermons were original, she says. He does not say what one expects, but has thoughts and teaching, which are striking - always calls things by their right names - allows no such thing as "a good sort of person on the whole," and speaks of things which man *likes*, but which God does not merely find disagreeable, or which he does not merely tolerate, but which are *abominations* to Him. Mr James, evidently, had no "fear of man which bringeth a snare." And, in spite of his outspokenness, he was in favour with both rich and poor.

In this same letter, Frances makes some far-seeing remarks about those who are fond of saying such things as, "I put my trust in God's mercy," and "trust in Providence." She always feels that there is something wrong; but if Jesus is spoken of - Jesus the Saviour - it always gave her a thrill.

And I think in this she was quite right. Often I have heard people speaking of "God's mercy," and so on, who would not seek His mercy in or through Christ His Son, the only way. There is a sort of idea of claiming God as Father by those who have no right to do so. We are children of God only when "born again" - children "by faith in Christ Jesus."

The letter goes on to state that she is probably going to stay under the same roof as the Prince of Wales - King Edward VII, then 16 years of age - at Konigswinter. Then she laughingly quotes: "If they'd only been a month forwarder, there would have been a collision" - in respect of the earth and the comet. In 1853 she had made the acquaintance of the Dowager Countess von Lippe, a relative of Prince

Albert's, with whom he had often spent his holidays from the University, and she expresses the wish to her correspondent that one of the Countess's daughters who was a princess, would come whilst she was there, as she had never spoken to a Princess!

She did speak to one eventually - the Princess Leonille Galitzin, of a Russian family. Miss Havergal, when she discovered the title of her new acquaintance, remarked that she herself had not title. The beautiful young princess, however, thought nothing of titles, and said she wouldn't have liked her young friend any more if she had one.

But there is a title we call should covet - an heir of God, and a joint-heir with Christ.

Later in the year (1857) she writes from Spa as having had a jolly summer till about September, and having become so "Germanized that she felt as if she belonged to them. The letter is concluded at home, St Nicholas Rectory, and she speaks of the crossing from Dover as a beautifully quiet passage, and so we see the frail wanderer at home again, and settled down for a time.

The years 1858 and 1859 were years of no particular incident.

I am trusting Thee, Lord Jesus,
Trusting only Thee,
Trusting Thee for full salvation,
Great and free.

I am trusting Thee for pardon,
At Thy feet I bow;
For Thy grace and tender mercy,
Trusting now.

I am trusting Thee for cleansing
In the crimson flood;
Trusting Thee to make me holy
By Thy blood.

I am trusting Thee to guide me:
Thou alone shalt lead,
Every day and hour supplying
All my need.

I am trusting Thee for power;
Thine shall never fail;
Words which Thou Thyself shalt give me
Must prevail.

I am trusting Thee, Lord Jesus;
Never let me fall;
I am trusting Thee for ever,
And for all.

CHAPTER FOUR
At Oakhampton

Frances and her friend, Elizabeth Clay, read and learned the Scriptures systematically, and Miss M.V.G. Havergal says that when she and her sister Frances were taking walks in the country, Frances would repeat alternate verses with her. She knew all the Gospels, Epistles, Revelation, the Psalms and Isaiah, and in later years she learnt the Minor Prophets. Such a remarkably retentive memory was a great gift, and was worthily used.

It goes without saying that her Sunday School preparation and teaching was a happy task. Her methodically kept Sunday school Register is in itself instructive. The birthday of each child was entered, the date of entrance into the Sunday School - occurrences in their homes - general impression of the character of each, and subsequent events in their lives are thoughtfully entered - a splendid, model, private Register for any Sunday school teacher. Perhaps some reader of these lines may be led to follow the example of F. R. H.

She had desperately uphill work with her scholars at one time. There were fourteen in her class, and only a few apparently were hopeful cases. But she struggled on, for she loved them dearly. She wept and prayed for them. Later, some of them would go to her for separate Bible reading, and for prayer. Those who were really anxious about the salvation of their souls found in her a confidante and friend.

When it came to the last page of her Register, which would never be filled - for the move to Shareshill was impending - she wrote a concluding note which shows her intense earnestness on their behalf. On reading it, one says, of course, "They that sow in tears shall reap in joy - he that goeth forth and weepeth, bearing precious seed, shall doubtless come again with rejoicing, bringing his sheaves with him."

The work had been a means of grace to her own soul, she says - and that often when prayer was cold and lifeless, the frozen stream would unseal in intercession for them, and she herself was blessed.

In 1860, when Miss Havergal was about twenty-four, her father resigned the living of St. Nicholas, where they had lived since 1845 and went to Shareshill, a quiet little country parish, more suited to his delicate state of health. The move was the cause of both sorrow and thankfulness to Frances. The fifteen years at St. Nicholas had been eventful ones to her. When first they moved there the child of nine missed the beauties of the country. Her father called her "a caged lark". She had loved the gardens and the long terrace walk there, and had indulged in tree climbing now and then. At St. Nicholas, Worcester, there were no such delights, but it became home to her eventually.

St. Nicholas held many sacred memories, and it was not to be wondered at that she felt some pangs of sorrow on leaving. But thankfulness on her father's account predominated. He had been very ill, but so bravely did he bear it that she declares it was thrilling to see him in it, so great was his peace, so grand his conception of God's sovereignty in all, and such quiet rejoicing in His will, no matter what it was; and such "shining trust" in Him.

At Shareshill, during her sojourn there, the Sunday delivery of mails was abolished. The inhabitants were unanimous in wishing for this. We can imagine how she rejoiced in the success. She intended to write on the subject, according to a list of the articles she made for 1879, but died before doing it.

Her testimony against the desecration of the Lord's Day would have been invaluable today.

In February of 1861, Miss Havergal went to her brother-in-law, Henry Crane, to teach their two little girls, Miriam and Evelyn. The arrangement met with her father's approval, for he knew that she would not be able to study so strenuously. She was about twenty-four years of age, her health was not of the best, but she was full of enthusiasm in the training of her young charges, and joined in all their amusements with zest. Sometimes they called her away from her own studies, no doubt with parental approval, possibly parental connivance (since she was ever tempted to study too much) and she wrote a sweet little poem, "The Children's Triumph" in which she shows, where the robin and the sunbeam failed, the children prevailed in getting her out into the glorious sunshine to play.

It was evident, however that F. R. H. Must be learning something. She speaks of how much can be learnt "in all the odds and ends of time" - a very valuable truth, not always realised or used.

She learnt the Italian verbs while her nieces were washing their hands for dinner, because she took five minutes less than they to be ready.

And she must have been very fond of learning languages. She knew German and French and now Italian is beginning. With her father and a friend she studied Hebrew and Greek, becoming sufficiently proficient in both to read the Scriptures in a scholarly as well as spiritual way - the spiritual always of course the most important.

During the years she spent at Oakhampton she was a regular contributor of hymns and poems to *Good Words* and other magazines.

Also she became a favourite solo singer at the Philharmonic Society, Kidderminister, where Dr. William Marsh, the conductor, was her teacher.

But her chief object was to teach her little nieces for Eternity, as well as time. It must have been about the year 1865 that she had the joy of leading one of them, Evelyn, to the Lord. Next year they both went to school, and their aunt returned to her parents at Shareshill, and moved with them, in 1867, to Leamington, where Mr. Havergal retired.

Evelyn had always been a sweet child and delicate.

In 1868, after a brief time a school, Evelyn died, and her death was a great grief to this loving aunt. She could not grasp the truth at first. But joy was there, too, the joy of assurance that they would meet again in the Father's House. Doubly glad she must have felt that it had been her privilege to lead this young niece to the Saviour.

In her poem, "The Two Rings", she describes little Evelyn, who was doing everything she could to postpone the trying business of going to bed, suddenly slipping Auntie's "Forget-me-not" ring on her own tiny finger - and the promise given by Auntie that it should some day be Evelyn's was understood by the child. She knew that when the ring became hers, Auntie would be on earth no longer. She cried, and said she hoped she would never wear it. Nor did she. But a little ring which belonged to Evelyn was sent to Auntie five years later, when the unexpected early Home-call came for the young niece.

Thy life was given for me,
Thy blood, O Lord, was shed
That I might ransomed be,
And quickened from the dead.
Thy life was given for me:
What have I given for Thee?

Long years were spent for me
In weariness and woe,
That through eternity
Thy glory I might know.
Long years were spent for me:
Have I spent one for Thee?

Thy Father's home of light,
Thy rainbow-circled throne,
Were left for earthly night,
For wanderings sad and lone.
Yea, all was left for me;
Have I left aught for Thee?

Thou, Lord, hast borne for me
More than my tongue can tell
Of bitterest agony
To rescue me from hell.
Thou sufferedst all for me:
What have I borne for Thee?

And Thou hast brought to me,
Down from Thy home above,
Salvation full and free,
Thy pardon and Thy love.
Great gifts Thou broughtest me:
What have I brought to Thee?

O let my life be given,
My years for Thee be spent;
World-fetters all be riven,
And joy with suffering blent;
To Thee my all I bring,
My Saviour and my King!

CHAPTER FIVE
The Visit to Hiller

In 1865 Miss Havergal went to Germany to visit her old friends the Schulze-Berges, and also stayed for a time with her parents at Bonn. Her friend, Miss Elizabeth Clay, had previously told the Schulze-Berges that Frances was composing, and during her visit they begged her to go to the Musical Academy at Cologne. This, she declares, was impossible, and then they suggested Hiller, in their opinion, the greatest living authority and composer. She must go to him, and show him her songs.

Her innate modesty caused her to shrink form this at first. She did not see how he could do anything but "quench" her, so little idea had she of her abilities - he, so great a man. Then she thought it better to know the worst, and if his verdict proved to be unfavourable, she would waste no more time over her compositions.

Mr. Havergal, too, urged her to go, much to her surprise. So she wrote to Hiller, who made an appointment promptly and kindly. She was accompanied by Mrs. Havergal, and they went by queer, narrow streets past the Rhine wharfs, where their droschky had difficulty in passing, out into the more open part where Hiller dwelt.

The sharp observant eyes of F. R. Havergal took in every detail - the small, quiet-mannered elderly man, of handsome Jewish physiognomy - his double room littered with music - the magnificent grand piano.

After a brief, polite greeting, he took her book of songs to read, giving her a volume of poems to look at by way of amusement, and then followed a long silence - he reading, she alternately furtively watching him, and glancing at her poetry book.

He read her song book three-quarters through, and then inquired what instructions she had had - what regular musical professor? When she said none he seemed scarcely able to believe her.

His verdict was very favourable. Her power of harmonisation astonished him and he gave her unlimited praise in that respect; at the same time telling her that her tunes bore the stamp of talent, not genius, but the talent, he assured her, was sufficient to make it advisable to devote herself to music. She should go to his friend Macfarren, in London, for she must not have a second rate teacher.

F.R.H. left him with much more encouragement and appreciation than she had expected, and after procuring the book on harmony which he recommend, she began its exercises with her accustomed energy.

Later on she wrote to a friend, Mary C-, saying she is steadily going through the book and enjoying it. She feels she has a sort of inherited instinct for harmonies, as no doubt she had, from her father. Her method of study, even before her visit to Hiller, was very unique. She kept a book on harmony in her bedroom and "in odds and ends of time" read enough to work out the exercises in her head before going to sleep. That the method was good, was abundantly proved by the difficulty she had in making Hiller believe that she had not had any special training.

Whilst at Oakhampton with her sister Miriam, Dr. Marshall, the conductor of the Philharmonic Concerts had often praised her musical powers, but she had never quite believed it, she says, because she thought, if it were so, she would feel cleverer than she did. Thus Hiller's verdict was the more astonishing to her, and she says to her friend that it would be affectation now, after his opinion, to say she had no talent. On the contrary, she means to develop and use it - use it far more than she dreamed at that time. She had been too shy to play for Hiller, but the interview with him gave her fresh impetus in her musical studies.

Her memory for music must have been wonderful, for she was able to play much of Handel, Beethoven, and Mendelssohn, without notes.

After the Hiller visit she went to friends in Lille - Monsieur and Madame V. They had about 270 nephews and nieces. 38 dined with them every Sunday. Monsieur ruled his large family circle with a firm hand, and he told her that he lectured them in an unforgettable manner when he saw anything of which he disapproved. A notable man - *"mon oncle Emile."*

The crossing from Calais this time was perfect - a glassy sea - and Miss Havergal leaned over the side of the boat watching the frothy waters behind the paddles.

She was, at this time, still at Oakhampton with her sister Miriam Crane, and teaching her two nieces Miriam and Evelyn. In one of her letters she speaks of rising early enough to have full time for prayer and Bible study. She found that if she did not get this in the early hours her prayers were hurried and formal and her mind full of other things. How true this is! Nothing makes up for that early tryst. Those of us who have the privilege of quiet and solitude at the beginning of the day do we consistently take advantage of it?

In April, May and June of this year (1866), Miss Havergal passed through a great trial - it does not transpire from the letters exactly what this trail was - but it was one which had to be borne alone, she said, humanly speaking, but it drew her more and more to find consolation in Christ.

Later, in July, at Lynton and Ilfracombe, came the joy of leading a friend out of a tangle of errors into the simplicity that is in Christ Jesus. And this was a healing balm to F. R. H. indeed. She stayed at Runnymede House in Ilfracombe.

Her health was very bad at this time, and there was not much "poetising." She was also prevented from doing many things she wished to so. Painful and dark were some of the days, but she comforted herself by thinking that they were fitting her as a helper of others who should travel a like path. She learned to sympathise with any who did.

She says in one of her letters that God's crosses are often made of very unexpected and strange material. Samuel Rutherford, two hundred years before, had said that our crosses would not bite upon us if we were heavenly minded.

Both these experienced saints meant God's crosses. But it is well for us if we have grace and wisdom to distinguish between God's crosses and those sorrows which we bring upon ourselves through disobedience and wilfulness. For the former we have need of His help in patient endurance - for the latter we need repentance and deep humility in bearing them - and the time will come when we shall be delivered. "Surely it is meet to be said unto God, I have borne chastisement. I will not offend any more." And the peaceable fruits of righteousness will follow.

There was one case of "poetising" despite her ill-health, and this is he "Welcome to Winterdyne," written for December 14th, 1866 ("Memorials of F. R. H.", Nisbet), when her sister Ellen Shaw, came from Ireland with her husband and children to reside there, near Bewdley. The lines are charming, simple and natural.

This change of residence made it possible for Miss Havergal to visit the family much more frequently.

Master, speak! Thy servant heareth,
Waiting for Thy gracious Word,
Longing for Thy voice that cheereth,
Master, let it now be heard.
I am listening, Lord, for Thee;
What hast Thou to say to me?

Speak to me by name, O Master,
Let me know it is to me;
Speak, that I may follow faster,
With a step more firm and free,
Where the Shepherd leads the flock
In the shadow of the Rock.

Master, speak! though least and lowest,
Let me not unheard depart;
Master, speak! for O Thou knowest
All the yearning of my heart;
Knowest all its truest need;
Speak, and make me blest indeed.

Master, speak! and make me ready,
When Thy voice is truly heard,
With obedience glad and steady
Still to follow every word.
I am listening, Lord, for Thee;
Master, speak! O speak to me!

CHAPTER SIX

Leamington

In some of her 1867 letters, written from different places during the time which elapsed between leaving her Oakhampton nieces, and settling down in Leamington, Miss Havergal has discussed several books with EC in a clear-headed simple manner which is most instructive.

Though she "disliked discussion", yet she hopes, when she sees her friend, to talk the book over, for it had exercised her very much. The book is too much for letter-discussion, she says, but she refers to the Fatherhood of God, with a summary of texts in which "Father" occurs, and shows why, rightly enough, she cannot accept "universal Fatherhood." She also pleads that any doctrine be given by the teacher with emphasis in the same proportion as it is given in God's Word, and that our teaching may be in accord with the mind of the Spirit.

Then, in another letter, about a "little book" - not named - one can see that her correspondent is impressed by the poisoned truths, the gilded errors, and "fair show in the flesh," referring in the last words to ritual ceremonies, and restoration of confession and cognate evils. FRH asks now it could possibly be expected that she would hold any other opinion of the book but this very unfavourable one.

After this criticism, follows the story of a little book called "The Blood of Jesus." It has brought peace to two hearts, and has been lent to someone else, with fear - fear which quickly turned to joy, for light shines into the heart of this friend (who has known nothing of the story of salvation) with such brightness that ever her very phraseology in religious things was a surprise to FRH; it was so Scriptural.

Following this, is shown, unconsciously, her skill with yet another friend, where she uses her musical talent as a "grappling iron," and eventually, after duet playing and so on, she boards the grappled little ship, to find a willingness to talk of spiritual things.

During the summer of this year (1867) she went to the Lakes with two friends, and writes that she had seen everything that was beautiful except snow. She saw Grassmere - Keswick - took a boat round Derwentwater - clambered up Lodore, and many other places - and "boated no end" on Lake Windermere.

This was her last year at Oakhampton, and she is very distressed that she has been a care and a burden when she wished to be the very opposite. Part of the time was spent at 1 Elizabeth Villas, Weston-super-Mare, whilst her mother was in Shrewsbury looking at houses, as Mr havergal was retiring from Shareshill.

From Weston-super-Mare, Miss Havergal writes to EC (who had recently lost her mother and has to make a change of residence) in a comforting way about the Lord searching out a resting place for His people to pitch their tents in.

Then comes an amusing little bit about a collection of everybody's hymns - *"Lyra Britannica"* in which her father's name and brief biography, etc., appears. There is one hymn by FRH in it, too, and she naively asks her friend to correct any copies she may see, as the editor had inserted *two* last verses, instead of choosing the one he liked best. FRH says it looks as if she possessed but one idea, and had to express it twice, in different words!

In a letter written from Pembridge Crescent, London, she says she wants to give singing lessons for the Church Missionary Society, and German Lessons for the Irish Society. Hoping to kill two birds with one stone as usual, she says it would give her "opportunities" with the members of her classes, and so it would. More of the "grappling iron" idea, as well as helping societies financially.

It appears that Miss Havergal never wastes a moment, and the active spirit was often too much for the frail body. One might think that she knew how short her life would be and so she filled her says to their utmost capacity.

She is very anxious to get her friend (Elizabeth) to join the YWCA Prayer union, then 2000 members. Evidently FRH at this time is conducting the weekly meeting of the Association in Leamington. Her YWCA membership card is dated, September 23rd, 1867. She remained a very live member to the end of her days.

In November, 1867, she writes of the east window in Mr Bickersteth's Church, Christ Church, Hampstead.

Before he came there, there had been much bitterness and controversy about the previous east window, which was eventually removed, and plain glass substituted. The bitterness still remained, but soon after the arrival of Edward Henry Bickersteth, his faithfulness and tact brought the feud to an end, and reconciled the opposing parties. When his first "little blossom" was taken there was a universal desire that he should renew the window and dedicate it to her.

The window is characteristic of the man in its simplicity and Christwardness. In the centre is a white scroll on blue ground, and on it the words, "Till He come," in crimson and gold. Nothing in the surrounding part to take the eye or the heart from those words: "Till He Come!" As he wrote:

> *Let the little while between,*
> *In the golden light be seen;*
> *Let us think how Heaven and Home*
> *Lie beyond that - "Till He Come!"*

Golden words, indeed! Countless thousands have been comforted by that hymn, as they have been by

> *Peace, perfect peace, in this dark world of sin?*
> *The blood of Jesus whispers peace within.*

In passing, we may note that it was Edward Henry Bickersteth who suggested to Anthony Norris Groves that he should go to Bagdad as missionary - no missionary ever having been obtained for that city. This was in 1829, seven years before Miss FR Havergal was born. Both these men have lived in Exeter, though not at the same time. I often pass the Bishop's Palace, and the site of Anthony N Groves' house on Northernhay, under the shadow of Athelstan's Tower. As far as I know, Miss Havergal never visited Exeter.

Edward Henry Bickersteth, whilst still at Christchurch, Hampstead, wrote to a friend, June 13th, 1879, referring to Miss Havergal's death. He says he had met her about April, in Elm Road, Hampstead, and she gave such a hearty and warm greeting. How little they knew that their next meeting would be in the presence of the Lord Whom both were serving so faithfully.

Staying at Godstone, just before she went down to Leamington, she writes of her birthday treat (on December 14th, her 31st birthday) as being a visit to the Zoological Gardens. It appears there was nothing in London she would rather see than that. She was, she says, a perfect baby about seeing animals. Immediately after that remark she says she managed to get three singing lessons. One might think she meant at the Zoo! However, she goes on to speak of Signor Randeggar, her tutor, and says he told her she could always count on singing expressively.

She must have been in a "poetising" mood, for she put all his instructions into rhyme, a most clever and amusing poem entitled: "My Singing Lesson" ("Memorials, FRH"). It is a pity one may not quote it in full, for it is so amusing, and full of useful hints. One, for instance (giving it in prose): The voice must never ring in the nasal cavity, as, if it did, no one would care for us to sing.

She was afraid the signor might resent this treatment of his lesson, but far from that - he begged a copy for his pupils! This lay on his table, not only to show to pupils, but to all professionals who visited him.

The Editor of the *Musical World* inserted the verses in his paper. Later Signor Randeggar asked Miss Havergal to write some verses which he might set to music. Twelve "Sacred Song for Little Singers" was the result.

In December, Mr Havergal retired, and he and his wife went to Pyrmont Villa, Leamington, where Frances joined them, as the two Oakhampton nieces were to go to school.

CHAPTER SEVEN

The Father's Home Call

Her first note from the new home, Pyrmont Villa, Leamington, is, presumably, written to her sister Marie, who edited "Memorials" and "Letters" of F.R.H., and Miss Frances Ridley Havergal is writing in her own room, wondering what kind of day she will go through in it.

Standing there, before she begins to write, she ponders on her beloved father's state of health, and unless she dies before he does, she realises that this room will be hers when the great sorrow which she knows is impending (his death) will have befallen her. Now she is praying the prayer which her own mother wished her to when FRH was only eleven: "Prepare me for all Thou art preparing for me." Thus the words which once fell on her deaf little ears and stubborn heart are now her earnest understanding petition to a loving Heavenly Father.

She tells all these thoughts to Marie, and goes on to say that in spite of them she has been feeling very ruffled, but always suffers for being naughty, and at once loses all enjoyment in prayer - the very best thing that can happen to one under the circumstances. A tender conscience soon leads one to 1 John 1:7, and shelter under the wings of love once more.

Her room is at the top of the house; its only drawback that she cannot use it for classes. She most emphatically declares that good carpets and furniture are devices to hinder usefulness. In act, she boyishly votes them a place at the bottom of the sea!

But, on the other hand, whilst visiting at Hilton Park, Great Malvern, she says she very much likes grand houses. She asks her correspondent if she could imagine FRH taking pleasure in beautiful staircases and that sort of thing. But of course she was not contemplating the use of Hilton Park for Bible Classes. If she had been, she would have viewed carpets, handsome staircases, etc. with a disapproving, not appreciating eye.

Leamington amazes her - "every hole and corner dusted out," but she is referring to the plentiful number of loving and keen workers. It would seem she despaired of finding a job for herself, but, of course, her niche was ready, as St Paul's Choir proved.

It was in April of this year that her much loved niece, Evelyn Crane, died, as mentioned earlier.

FRH visited London and speaks of hearing Spurgeon one Sunday, and it had been a time of intense delight. She heard him in the morning, and in the evening she went to Westminster Abbey, where the sermon seemed cold and argumentative. She did, however, have the pleasure of hearing one of her father's chants most beautifully rendered on this occasion.

Of Spurgeon's Tabernacle she speaks enthusiastically - that with London half empty *it* was *thronged*, and with a preponderance of men - *intellectual* looking men. Yes, thank God, many intellectual men had discovered that the "natural man" needs the power of the Spirit of God to enable them to discern spiritual things, and thus it was that the Tabernacle was filled with those humble ones who yearned to know the things of God which their own intelligence could never teach them, for "they are spiritually discerned."

In May, 1869, thirteen months after the death of her niece, Evelyn, she went to Switzerland with her sister Mirian Crane, Mr Crane, and their daughter Miriam. There she revelled in her first sight of snow-covered mountains.

When she was quite a little girl (only eight years old) she used to think about them, one especially Siena de la Somma Pay (Perfect peace). Eternal snow and perfect peace had always been linked together in her mind. She was not disappointed in her first view, or her later ones. Snow mountains in her thoughts led up to the Unseen, they suggested to her the very steps of the Throne; and in this realisation of the things which are not seen, she lost sight of the fact that it was merely snow and granite rising out of the every-day earth - for "the City which hath foundation, whose builder and maker is God," filled her thoughts.

Autumn of this year found her in Scotland, enjoying the scenery in the Highlands. And the months sped away until 1870 was passing - the last precious months she would spend with her beloved father.

His help and understanding in her studies were a dear delight. What bliss to fly into his library and discuss her tunes and poems with him - to tell him her thoughts.

Then came the blow. On Easter even he spent a happy day, apparently unusually well, composing a tune in the morning, and then had a walk, after which he played the tune to her on his harmonium. Also he chatted with several friends, and there as no foreshadowing of the coming end.

FRH was out to tea that day, but got home at 8.30pm, in time for prayers. She went to fetch something immediately after, and on returning to the room again she found that her father had retired to bed. Knowing he was weary, she did not run up to his bedroom to say "Good night" she did not guess that she would not have a kiss from him again. The stroke laid him low about six the next morning, Easter Sunday, April 17th, and he never regained consciousness. There was no pain, no struggle, when on the following Tuesday the call came. He simply ceased breathing, and passed into the presence of his Lord.

The day after his passing, FRH wrote to inform their friends in Snepps, and begs that she may have the copy of the last tune he wrote on the Saturday before he died. It was in his very own handwriting, and he and FRH had discussed some trifling alterations. Also, it was the last time he had played to her. She named this tune "Havergal (163 Havergal's Psalmody). He was buried in Astley Churchyard - having chosen the spot years before, under the fir tree, "until the day break and the shadows flee away."

Miss Frances Ridley Havergal says she does not know how to express the great grief her mother felt - but no murmuring. Her care of her husband, and the devotion which had often warded off illness was now unavailing. His passing must have left a very great void in the poor wife's life, and caused rather a breakdown in various ways, making her somewhat difficult, perhaps, as the years went by. But, nevertheless, she did not sorrow - neither did Frances - as those who have no hope. He was at Home with the Lord, whither their feet, too, were tending.

Miss Havergal speaks of two visits to his grave in July. One was made in company with her mother, who was so overcome that the poor daughter was unable to have a moment of quiet meditation, her attention being given entirely to Mrs Havergal. But, she says, she slipped away to Astley churchyard again on Monday evening, and experienced wonderful peace; she was hardly even sad, she writes.

Thank God, one knows that this is possible. When one has stood alone at the foot of a love one's last earthly resting place and been enabled to look up - to remember "Perhaps today".

Perhaps to-day the Glad surprise -
The winging through the air!

In Shareshill and St Nicholas Churches, as also in Worcester Cathedral, there are memorial tablets to Mr Havergal.

Like a river glorious
Is God's perfect peace,
Over all victorious
In its bright increase;
Perfect yet it floweth
Fuller every day;
Perfect, yet it groweth
Deeper all the way.

Stayed upon Jehovah
Hearts are fully blest,
Finding, as He promised,
Perfect peace and rest.

Hidden in the hollow
Of His blessed hand,
Never foe can follow,
never traitor stand;
Not a surge of worry,
Not a shade of care,
Not a blast of hurry
Touch the spirit there.

Every joy or trial
Falleth from above,
Traced upon our dial
By the Sun of Love:
We may trust Him fully
All for us to do;
They who trust Him wholly
Find Him wholly true.

CHAPTER EIGHT

Switzerland with E.C.

Shortly after her father's Home-call, Miss Havergal undertook the editing of "Havergal's Psalmody" for the press, a task for which she was eminently qualified. The sympathy and fellowship she had had with her father gave her real understanding of his works, and her natural gift of harmonising was, of course, invaluable.

But even to one so gifted it was a difficult task. Feeling the weight of it, and the need of his help, she realised one day in its full force, the text: "Thou art the Helper of the fatherless," when she had it in her morning reading. It was the first orphan promise, and she claimed it with rejoicing. From that time she felt that the Lord was her Helper in the work.

In one of her letters it was easy to see that it was a great disappointment not to be allowed to put even her initials at the end of the preface. It was anonymously edited.

Mrs Havergal did not wish Frances to put her name, and, naturally, Frances was puzzled as to why, when she had already published "The Ministry of Song" under her own name, with her father's express approval. She was, however, too gentle to stand out for her own wishes, though she felt she was losing an advantage in doing so.

But whatever her own disappointments or troubles, she was able to sympathise with the sorrows of her friends. Mrs Snepp lost her seven-month-old baby at this time. The day before he passed away he fixed his eyes upon his mother with a longer gaze of wonderful intelligence and love, and after repeated efforts spoke one word, "Mama". It was Mrs Snepp's third loss in that year. FRH wrote a sweet letter and verse to the bereaved mother, for she could not pass over such a trial, even though her time was so filled.

In fact she was a renowned comforter. "Frances' lady loves" became quite a joke among her friends - and included at this time the young wife of the Rector of a very large parish, and we doubt not, as a clergyman's daughter, FRH was an excellent counsellor.

In June 1871, Miss Havergal and her friend Elizabeth Clay went to Switzerland. They had only carpet bags (no neat little attache cases in those days) and knapsacks. In fact they were "hiking" as we like to call it now, and were able to follow other paths than the beaten routes.

Her letters about this tour are very lively and descriptive. One can feel "on the spot," as she writes from the Peak of Gorner Grat, 10,200 feet up - 9am - and they had started from Riffel at 3am. They had to walk up and down, and round and round a space of three or four yards in order to keep warm, till six, when the sun had gained power. Snow all round, frozen hard - but at 9am it was quite hot - not a cloud, every peak standing out in glittering snowy dress against the deep blue of the sky.

After that came a breakfast brought up by the guide - bread, hard-boiled eggs, and wine.

They were always up before five, sometimes before four. She declares that hymn-writing was impossible, there was need to look at every step; there are also distractingly lovely flowers, and hosts of other lovely things - concentration was impossible. And presently follows an amusing remark that a Switzerland holiday is very different from "messing about" at the seaside in England! (Later she managed to enjoy this, too, for she visited Weston-super-Mare).

The two friends felt like children, and except for the undercurrent of praise were in the wildest of spirits.

Their experiences in the Italian valleys, to which they went later during their tour, were interesting., She speaks of the Vaudois Missionary pastor at Courmayeur, Costabel by name. He was very isolated, his principal friends being the English Chaplain and his wife, Mr and Mrs Phinn. The pastor told them that the fear of death was awful amongst the people there. He was often present at the most painful death scenes. All their lives they are satisfied to leave everything to the priests, believing he can make it all right for them at the end. The only thing they trouble about is compliance with certain forms, but when they are dying they realise that the priest's powers are unavailing. They seek peace and have none; they wish for assurance, but they die in terror. Poor, deluded souls! Are there not hundreds such in our own land?

It was only the poor who would listen to the pastor, and those in the outlying villages where priestly dominance was not so great. Miss Havergal and her friend found the people quite different from the Swiff - more cautions in accepting Gospels. "Protestant book?" they would ask, but generally were prevailed upon, ultimately, to take them.

Writing from Chapiu, she gives a pretty description of a meeting with a number of Italians who, like themselves were going up the Col de la Seigne for the day. FRH and her friends picnicked at the top, and, having finished were moving off when the party seated at a little distance all rose and expressed a wish to drink a toast with them before they left. There was no refusing so friendly a request, and *"Vive l'Angleterre"* was very enthusiastic. Miss Havergal and her friend responded with *"Viva l'Italia,"* which pleased them. After which an old priest inquired if they were Catholics, and suggested *"Viva Roma!"* FRH wisely replied that they could at least say *"Viva Roma, capitale d'Italia,"* to which he added: *"Viva Christianity,"* and FRH and her friends smilingly and heartily agreed. This incident took place at the boundary between France and Italy, close to the cross which marks it.

Miss Havergal, in a letter from Zermatt to the wife of a clergyman, says how thankful she is that she is coming to them when the Swiss tour is over, instead of going direct to Pyrmont Villa. There is no beloved father there to whom she could recount her experiences. On the occasion of a former visit to Switzerland she had stored up everything she could to tell him. How different now! Ah, that first time - to go back to the familiar home, and see the empty chair!

At Zermatt she had been reading the Bible every day with a girl, a young Swiss waitress, and she is beginning to get free of her Romish idea that good works will save her from going to purgatory and merit Heaven. FRH says how welcome the news of *free* salvation was to the poor little thing.

Next we find her at Oakhampton enjoying three quiet days with no one, not even her relatives, about her. Her sister Miriam had told the servants of the probable arrival of Frances, so they were not surprised. Miss Havergal had much ado to assure them that five sitting rooms were not necessary to her comfort.

Oakhampton had a flat roof, from whence she could view the lovely surroundings, and one Sunday morning she spent up there, not being well enough to go to the distant church.

The Christmas of this year was sad to Miss Havergal - the first Christmas without her father. It was her second return to Pyrmont Villa since his death, and she found it as trying as the first. But with her usual wisdom, she determined to dwell more on Christmas mercies than her sorrow. Her sister Maria was able to come to Pyrmont Villa, which helped to pass the sad evening, which could not but recall him vividly to FRH and her poor stricken stepmother.

In one of her letters she speaks pathetically of looking forward to the milder days of spring, so that she can use her study every day, instead of only one day a week. Mrs Havergal would not agree to a fire there more than once a week, though FRH had offered to pay for the coals, and pay for the extra trouble. This must have been a sore trial. One can understand that to concentrate the mind on anything in a room likely to be invaded by numerous callers was quite impossible - and, consequently, on the study fire-day she worked too hard. Mrs Havergal can have no conception of what she was making her dutiful step-daughter endure. And FRH was thirty-five years of age by this time - and by her talents independent financially. It was a surprising and difficult state of things, and one would have thought that the mother might yield. But it looks as though her great sorrow had hardened, and, perhaps, soured Mrs Havergal a little. As Mrs Barter Snow says in "Cared for, and Carried": "He cannot trust all with sorrow, for some it would only harden … Oh sorrowful one, let Jesus carry you across the sea of sorrow."

They were never at home in the summer, so the study was then used perhaps very unconcernedly by someone else, or more probably, left empty. If it was cold under the slate roof during winter (the study was at the top of the house), it would be exceedingly hot all day in summer.

Well - some day -

We'll know why clouds instead of sun
Were over many a cherished plan.
Why song has ceased, ere scarce begun -
Up there - some day - we'll understand.

CHAPTER NINE

Marie and Frances in Wales

 The year 1872 was a year of which Miss Havergal says "it was a series of little successes and great mercies."

She was beginning to sow the Gospel seed among laundry girls, by visiting the laundry itself. She related "the old, old story of Jesus and His love" in the big working hall. Here and there an iron was stayed, and everywhere silence prevailed, and several of her hearers were in tears. Who knows what harvest resulted?

Then, at a fashionable school she is giving "mild lectures" on Psalmody - just the "grappling iron" again.

She wrote: "Tell it out among the heathen that the Lord is King," which caught on well everywhere, in May of this year, as well as a plea in verse for the use of the Bible in schools.

Her little book "Bruey" was published about this time, and later translated into French, to become a favourite in the schoolroom. It was dedicated to two little nieces, Alice and Bertha. "Bruey" was Miss Havergal's first collector in the city of Worcester for the Irish Society - a little girl, one whose name was Bruce - pet name "Bruey". The story of her brief life, her collecting for the Irish Society and her Sunday School, as well as her peaceful death, make a touching narrative. A branch of the Irish Society members was called the "Bruey" branch.

This year, among the mercies recorded, Miss Havergal and her beloved sister Marie went to Wales together. FRH recovered health and buoyancy there, and they had a wonderful time in those few weeks. Barmouth, Pen-y-gard, and Moel Siabod were among the places visited, and on the top of Snowdon FRH used her facile pen to indict a letter to her friend Miss Elizabeth Clay. She says her sister has the scent of a Red Indian for good old widows, and people who needed consolation. One might of course idly remark that Red Indians were not much given to that sort of thing, but this brief glimpse of Marie's activities is interesting. MVGH deserves a "Memorial" herself. And FRH finds it sweet to tell this sister things she could not write. There was evidently a strong bond between all the four daughters of Mr Havergal, for FRH in one of her letters expresses amusement that the friend to whom she is writing should fear any objection on Miriam's part when FRH went to stay at Oakhampton during her sister's absence. She says that each sister honestly liked each of the others to do exactly what they pleased.

In the Snowdon letter to Miss Elizabeth Clay, FRH says she had received 600 letters from January to July 1st. So great and varied was her correspondence that she was obliged to have a circular printed, answering the many different questions she was repeatedly asked. She simply marked the paragraph which applied to the question, or questions, and sent it off. This is not so indifferent as it may sound, for the circular began with a few lines, expressed in her daintiest way, of apology for not writing a letter.

This year, on account of their being in Wales at the time, she missed the Mildmay Conference, but writes very cheerfully about it, "Among Foxgloves and Ferns, Dolgelly." The sisters were very early birds, up and out before 8am. Taking their dinner with them one day, they remained for hours on a Cader Idris, and the valley down to Barmouth, sea and mountain, and "Sal Volatile air".

FRH says that during this visit she was allowed to lead several souls to the Saviour.

At the end of July they were at home again for the wedding of their niece, Miriam Crane.

At this time Miss Havergal was getting on with her volume of poems, "Under the Surface" (Nisbet & Co.). "The Ministry of Song" was published in 1869. "Under the Surface," she says, would be one fourth larger.

In the summer of 1873, Miss Havergal went to Switzerland with Mr and Mrs Snepp and their daughter Emily. Her letters describe her climb up the Grand Mulets on Mont Blanc, and their stand beside the snow-surrounded desolate-looking rocks, and the sun shining through colossal blocks of ice, wonderfully iridescent.

FRH loved glissading, and she loved not to be roped. These two things led to almost catastrophe when on this expedition to Mont Blanc. The party reached Pierre l'Echelle. FRH was not allowed to be unroped there, as it is evident that she had hoped to be, but she was enjoying glissades very much - too much - for, thinking they were at a place easy enough to be careless in, she slipped, pulled down the guide, and they both headed for a black chasm, down a steep incline. Mr Snepp, with very commendable presence of mind, flung himself on his back, stuck his heels deep into the snow, and hung on, thus checking the two who were slipping, just in time - practically saving the lives of all the party by that cool, courageous act.

FRH says that after that she was unroped, and enjoyed some glassades alone - the party arriving at Chamouix in less time than usual. No doubt the guide and the Snepps were thankful to arrive without further mishap.

In this incident FRH shows herself humanly wayward and headstrong. She must have been a great responsibility in such moods. She speaks later in a letter, of her thankfulness in having lost all sense of the excitement which she had felt while in Switzerland, with its following depression and anxiety taken away. She had not, she affirms, the same deep desire for Christ during the 1872 tour, as when with Elizabeth Clay. And she gives thanks for being "restored, and feeling happy in Jesus."

Mrs Havergal was at the seaside when FRH returned from Switzerland, so she went to Oakhampton, where her diligence soon resulted in a big gathering in the servants' hall. After this she went to Winterdyne, Bewdley, her sister Ellen's home, from where she assisted in a very memorable mission at Bewdley. The Winterdyne people were specially blessed at this time.

Mr Snepp undertook the services, and Miss Havergal was very busy choir-training, and speaking, and seeking. There was a great and blessed harvest, and words which FRH spoke to anxious souls were, in many cases, most distinctly remembered long after she had passed away. This was proved by MVGH herself, in 1885, when repeating a text to a dying woman. The dear soul told her "they were the last words Miss Frances said to me." Among the choirboys, too, were many and sweet recollections of Miss Havergal in that mission, and many young lives were yielded to the Saviour.

Later on she was helping in a mission in Liverpool, which taxed her strength sorely. "Little Pillows" and "Morning Bells" she found were very useful and acceptable to those in charge of children. She bemoans the fact that so many Christians do not try to be soul-winners, and she wonders when they can talk so charmingly of other things, that they do not speak about their Lord and Saviour.

Against this moan she puts the incident of a lady who found a tract by FRH in an Edinburgh street entitled: "Have you not a word for Jesus?" and who, after reading it, determined that henceforth she would speak for Him. This lady even took the trouble to write and tell FRH, which greatly cheered her.

In a letter written to Miss Elizabeth Clay, December 1873, she refers to Elizabeth's growing deafness, and says she knows no trial from which she would shrink so much. But she sends the lovely verses, "From Glory unto Glory" to EC, emphasising the line: "Whatever lies before us, there can be nought to fear."

She wrote this poem at Winterdyne, after a great spiritual experience, an experience which caused her peace and joy exercise, her sister says, and there were no more dark ravines.

It was in this year that Mr Snepp, who had saved her from that bad slip on Mount Blanc, now saved her from a bad slip in the spiritual sense. She was staying at Perry Villa when Dr Marshall, the conductor of the Philharmonic

Concerts sent her the programme of the next one to be held at Kidderminster. He also begged her to take the part of Jezebel in "Elijah" for he had no one who could do it so well. FRH knew she was quite equal to it. She had practised it once before, and Dr Marshall had been struck by her rendering.

She mentioned it to Mr Snepp, and he quietly asked her how a Christian woman could personate Jezebel?

Miss Havergal found that quiet question enough. Dr Marshall did not have his wish gratified, and that further couplet was added to her consecration hymn:

Take my voice and let me sing,
Always, only, for my King.

CHAPTER TEN

Witnessing Here and There

In one of her 1874 letters, written March 31st, to a friend of her sister Marie, she affords a glimpse of MVGH. The friend, Mrs Edward Pease, has sent a Tyrolean shawl to FRH. In thanking her, FRH says they could not really be strangers, though they had never met, as they loved the same dear Saviour. And, moreover, Marie had so often talked of her that FRH felt as though she already knew Mrs Peace. Then she speaks her gratitude for the help given by Mrs E Pease to Marie, by supporing a nurse for Marie's sick poor. There was nothing, she says, which could have given such great help; and all those who loved Marie and had been fearing that she would have a breakdown are most grateful for the relief which the nurse afforded. And so we see something of the life work of MVGH, and of the appreciation of that work shown by others.

Early in this year, Miss Frances Ridley Havergal was expecting a letter from America with money due to her.

"Bruey" the little life-story, she hoped was going on well, and the book of poems "Under the Surface" then being compiled, was very eagerly expected across the Atlantic by the American publishers. Instead of this comes news of the publisher's submersion in the torrent of a universal failure. Moreover, he held her written promise to publish out there with none but himself, on consideration of his giving her a start in America.

On receipt of the news she felt that all American prospects were over. And yet, though the loss looked overwhelming, she emerged joyfully. God lifted her above it all in a new and wonderful way, such as she had never known before.

She says tha if she had lost her English standing and prospects as well, it would have been worth wile for the joy she felt at the manifestation of His faithfulness and power. "So true to all His promises" Yea and Amen, indeed.

Such opportunity has perhaps been given to us to prove our Lord's faithfulness. Did we use it to such good purpose? There may possibly be some such opportunity in store for us yet. Shall we glorify Him in it? Shall we take the real chance of trusting Him? We shall surely find, as Miss Havergal did, that it is worth while to suffer loss if we have the greatest gain of a deep and abiding joy in Him Who can sustain us through all.

How tenderly must that question have sounded in the ears of His disciple: "When I sent you without purse, and script, and shoes, lacked ye anything? And how emphatic the brief reply: "Nothing." Contrast this with yet another question: "Can God furnish a table in the wilderness?" What querulous unbelief. How often had He proved His power to provide, and defend, and yet -. Let us see that we do not fall into the same faithlessness.

> *His love in times past forbids me to think*
> *He'll leave me at last in trouble to sink;*
> *Each sweet Ebenezer I have in review*
> *Confirms His good pleasure to help me quite through.*

In one of her letters to a young convert, CH, she writes her letter in question form, commenting thus on CH's letter to her. Here is the gist of her letter:

Presumption, to speak for Jesus! Is a soldier presumptuous to say what a good general he has? Is it presumption for a liberated slave to tell of his deliveries to his one-time fellow-slaves?

She herself would speak for Him anywhere and everywhere, and *sing* for Him in the most unlikely places. At the first big gathering she went to in Leamington she was asked to sing, and she sang: "Whom having not seen ye love."

Everyone was greatly astonished, and there was a profound silence whilst she was singing, a silence not easily broken when she had finished. Two Christian girls were among her audience, and afterwards they told her that they did not know music and singing could be used in the service of the Lord Jesus Christ. After a talk with Miss Havergal, they made up their minds to put more vigour into their wearisome daily practice, and so fit themselves for this form of service.

At a London "party" she says she felt the secret of His Presence, and sang to the glory of God. The room was a large double one, and filled with people. Dead silence, of course, and no doubt some very uncomfortable moments, but afterwards she found herself conversing with two strangers as a result. One of them began with light badinage, but soon, in a quiet corner of that room, he found he was facing life's most solemn question - that of his soul's salvation. When he came to that party he certainly had not anticipated such a thing. He had never given a thought to any after-life.

Her courage in singing spiritual songs, and in this gentle "cornering", and her wisdom when challenged, were God-given. And, above all, she believed that her song would touch hearts only if she was looking up to Him, and seeking *His* blessing, *His* approbation alone.

During this London visit she was taken to see Dore's pictures, which she enjoyed immensely. One can imagine her standing in front of "The Ascension" thinking of "this same Jesus" Who will return again. She also went to see her music publishers - had tea with them at their business house, and sung some of her tunes and hymns to them. One of the gentlemen sang as well - in fact, they had quite a pleasant little concert together.

At Bocking Parsonage she had several meetings in four days, and at this time an incident of much interest occurred. She was at Bishop Stortford, in the train, being "seen off" by a young friend, when a gentleman in the carriage asked some question about the place, adding that he hoped to have meetings there for children.'

Miss Havergal was sharp enough to guess that this gentleman was Mr. Spiers, and, in her turn, asked him many questions. He then discovered, when she gave him her little leaflet, "From Glory to Glory," to whom he was talking, and was much pleased to make her acquaintance. Before he discovered her identity, he had asked what *her* work was, to which she had replied in effect that it was anything that came along, a reply which was full of meaning when he knew her for F.R.H.

She went to Switzerland this year with her niece, Constance Crane, and other friends joined them in their mountain climbing.

Miss Havergal, as usual, sends vivid descriptions by letter. The wonder is she never took up the brush, for she had the artist's eye and pen! She remarks in a letter to her mother that she might "go on for sheets" describing what seemed a glimpse of heavenly heights.

This was when they stood to watch the sunset on the Faulhorn. Such a scene would naturally carry such a mind to the "sweet and blessed country, the Home of God's elect," and cause a catching of the breath as that loveliness met her view. Her heart would be full of the things not seen - so lovely that they have not entered into the heart of man. What will the sight be of that City where:

> The Lamb is all thy splendour,
> The Crucified thy praise?

At one time they all saw their shadows thrown in enormous size on a cloud surrounded by rainbow hues. Of course, being of one mind, they had to sing as they watched the wonderful colour-pageant (it remained nearly one hour), "Abide with me, fast falls the eventide," and "Glory to Thee, My God, this night."

In the second month of this tour she put idleness out of the first place, and began to write, but in small doses. As she remarks, four or five hours' good work could be done there, and still one could spend half the day in the open air. One morning she repaired to a quiet spot near a stream, prepared to write a poem on "The Thoughts of God." She prayed first that if He had anything else for her to do she might be willing - she was willing - and instead of writing the poem that morning she was required to tell "the old, old story of Jesus and His love" to several people.

The first was a labourer. He came along with his scythe, just as the poem had attained the length of four lines, to drink at the nearby stream.

Miss Havergal called him, and offered him a little book, and he, instead of going on, sat down to look at it, and she talked to him. He seemed responsive, but was just moving off when his two boys burst through the bushes to sit beside him and listen, so he sat down again.

She did not, it seems, actually bring them to the point, but at least they had heard, and then they went off. Miss Havergal was once more engaged on her poem, when the younger boy came back with his seventeen year old sister. Not speaking a single word to Miss Havergal, they both sat down beside her, and she forthwith began to talk to them. They stayed for half an hour, and she had great hopes that the seed sown would spring up to everlasting life.

And so the morning for poem writing passed away, and the inspiration vanished too!

Thus it was from day to day, here a little and there a little, she spoke, seeing the fruit of her labours now and then, but content to leave the seeing, or the not-seeing to her Lord. Some people discourage themselves by looking for results and seeing none. Better far to work on, earnestly and honestly, and to remember that "God giveth the increase."

Miss Havergal was carrying out injunctions given to a friend - injunctions to be willing to do any "odds and ends of work" which the Saviour put before her.

Odds and ends of work! Some of us have visions of great pieces of work for ourselves on His behalf, and are not content to do His small behests. Odds and ends of work, and odds and ends of time were of great value to Miss Havergal.

It was during this tour she finished "Little Pillows" and "Morning Bells" for the press. What thousands of homes those little books have entered. I wonder, do the readers think of the diligent author writing out her pure messages amidst the snowcapped mountains and by a rippling stream?

On one occasion two of Cook's tourists asked her to interpret something for them, which she did, and then they "drifted" into spiritual talk on Christ's finished work. One of them said, in assured, quiet tones, that Christ takes our sins and gives us His righteousness. It is a transfer. Then he spoke of an invalid Irish clergyman whom they had met on the Rigi, and said it was he who had so clearly shown them this truth. Banished through ill health from his church, he was sowing the seed in many places. And thus, on the Rigi, the Englishman from London heard the glorious news of substitution - of the transfer - as he called it.

The Good Shepherd had indeed sought this wandering sheep until He found it.

God moves in a mysterious way
His wonders to perform.

Precious, precious blood of Jesus
Shed on Calvary;
Shed for rebels, shed for sinners,
Shed for thee!

Precious, precious blood of Jesus,
Ever flowing free;
O believe it; O receive it,
'Tis for thee.

Precious, precious blood of Jesus,
Let it make thee whole;
Let it flow in mighty cleansing
O'er thy soul.

Though thy sins are red like crimson,
Deep in scarlet glow,
Jesus' precious blood shall wash thee
White as snow.

Precious blood that hath redeemed us!
All the price is paid;
Perfect pardon now is offered;
Peace is made.

Now the holiest with boldness
We may enter in;
For the open fountain cleanseth
From all sin.

Precious blood! by this we conquer
In the fiercest fight,
Sin and Satan overcoming
By its might.

Precious blood, whose full atonement
Makes us nigh to God!
Precious blood, our way of glory,
Praise and laud!

CHAPTER ELEVEN

A Year of Suffering and Silence

In England once more, and among daily duties, Miss Havergal pursues the trivial round, so-called, and in her accustomed energetic way. Letters have still a way of pouring in, and her advice is asked on many questions, and wherever possible a personal reply is given.

She writes a letter at this time to one who was starting her career as a governess soon after leaving school.

Miss Havergal is glad and thankful that this young pilgrim's first post, away from her own home and her own mother, is where there is sweet spiritual atmosphere. There are not so many governesses now as at this time (about 1875), for children go to school more. But the advice holds good still.

Here are the principal points.

Show children from the outset that what you say *must* be done.

Be very careful in what you say. When once you've said it, carry it through.

If you are not *sure* that a thing has to be done, don't say it must be - or there will be the humiliating necessity of giving in, or retracting.

Ask to have your supper upstairs, so that you have time for self-improvement, practising, reading, and so on.

Don't allow children to be inconsiderate to anyone.

Never let them impose on yourself or on others.

Don't let the maids thing you stuck up. Be pleasant, gentle, and kind to them. Always thank them nicely for their service.

Study their convenience and they will study yours.

Pray for God's special blessing on your work, yourself, your pupils and all around; for nothing prospers without prayers.

Keep your colours flying.

I may say, that for a short time this particular young teacher needed a little bolstering up, but she was evidently very young, and would improve. F. R. H. Was very patient with her, and very understanding.

Late this year Miss Havergal was very ill. It was when she was returning homeward after a series of visits. Ill though she felt with sickness and headache, she bravely fulfilled a promise to her sister Marie to meet a girl in Willesden Station, and stay with her there for an hour, to talk with her. The girl, some how, did not arrive at the specified time, so Miss Havergal, when an hour and a half had elapsed was unable to stay longer. Just as she was leaving, the object of her solicitude hurried into the station, and Miss Havergal took her some miles in the train in order to have the promised interview.

The words spoken were helpful. The girl was much moved, and so glad that she had once at least, seen the peaceful, satisfied face of F.R.H. It seems they never met again.

When Miss Havergal reached home, shivering set in, and in a short time it was discovered that she was suffering from typhoid fever. Doctors, trained nurses, and all the loving care of sisters and mother could not avert the attack. In November they were wondering which it would be - life or death.

Then the tide slowly turned, and she came back from the very gates of Heaven, it seemed, to take up her earthly life once more. There followed a recovery, very slow, with many a backward look. She told M.V.G.H. afterwards that she was very happy - that her mother's love and tenderness, day and night, could not be exceeded.

But about the middle of January 1875, a change of air was advised and her sister marie took her to Winterdyne, the home of their sister Ellen (Mrs. Shaw).

Just as the invalid was being helped into the carriage at her Leamington home preparatory to being conveyed to Winterdyne, a telegram arrived containing the news of their brother Henry's death. They did not tell F. R. H. until the journey to her sister's was over.

Gently though they did so, the shock brought on a relapse and for many weeks longer she was ill.

The dear mother was there much of the time, for both F. R. H. and M.V.G. H. knew how wise she was in illness, and how well her judgment could be trusted. Her handiness and her keen watchfulness were of incalculable service.

On the day of Mrs. Havergal's arrival, Frances told her she was trusting the Saviour all the way, and the mother made answer that He would not lead them so far by the right way and then leave them. She knew He would see them through.

Marie, in one of her conversations with Frances, says that when we first see Him in Heaven it will be alone, and F. R. H. refers to "Yesterday, today and forever" by Bishop Bickersteth: when the Seer and the Saviour meet, the angel leaves the Seer to advance alone.

Whether we see Him first alone or not, we will surely have no eyes or thought for anyone else.

Miss Havergal was soon writing letters. She was very happy at Winterdyne. It always appeared to her as a sort of "Millennial household".

She writes in one of her letters from there that "Bells" and "Pillows" are a great success as regards the number sold. For a computation of spiritual success, we know, she would have to wait for "the day to declare".

In another letter she says the wonders if this year (1875) was her pilgrimage's halfway house - and if so, what the other half would be. She did not know that in a little over four brief years she would be in the presence of her Lord. She comments, in this same letter, on the hymn:

"O Lord, how happy should we be,
If we could cast our care on Thee -"

wondering that she ever thought it charming.

I think she forgets how very difficult she herself found it at times prior to this, to cast her care on Him. People do sometimes argue from the greater height of experience and long practise, forgetting that in days gone by they so often were nearly - but-just-not-doing the things which come so easily to them now.

Another hymn, or verse of it, she comments on unfavourably:

> *"If I find Him, if I follow,*
> *What His guerdon here?*
> *Many a sorrow, many a labour,*
> *Many a tear."*

She can't think how any Christian can sing it. She asks, "Where did He say that was His guerdon?"

Well, we know that He said, "In the world ye shall have tribulations," and we may not always rise to the "Be of good cheer". We know that His Word says: "If any will live godly in Christ Jesus he shall suffer persecution." And we may often shed tears in those suffering, and feel sorrow - "many a sorrow" - over those who can so persecute us, and who will not come to Him that they might have life. I think He has bid us be prepare for "many a sorrow, many a labour, many a tear" in His happy service here. But there will be joy and peace bedsides. There is joy unspeakable and full of glory in our hearts even when sorrow is in our cup.

In April she writes to a friend (the late Mary Shekleton) that all her writings seem to have been more abundantly blessed than ever. 8000 of "Little Pillows" and "Morning Bells" were sold in less than two months.

To an American friend, Mrs. Brund, she writes that God has carried on her work here, that her books and leaflets have been widely circulated, and with much blessing.

At this time Messrs. Moody and Sankey were in Dublin, and Mr. Sankey prayed for F. R. H. there is one of their meetings, during this dreadful 1875 illness. And all over the country, too, prayer was made for this loved poetess and author.

Though this illness Miss Havergal says she was fully shown that seeming hindrances proved in God's good plan, to be helps to His work, and as delicacy precluded any definite work on her part, she was always on the look out for any He was pleased to send her. And she feels that she was allowed to do more for Him in this way then she could have in her own.

After spending January to April at Winterdyne, she was advised a change of air again, and soon found herself happily established at Oakhampton.

At Winterdyne and Oakhampton the servants were devoted to her and her addresses in their hall were much appreciated. All those at Oakhampton became members of the Christian Progress Union.

In a letter dated about May oft his year, she says all verse has gone from her, as it did once before for five years. But when she went to Whitby in the autumn she had the power again and wrote a beautiful poem of nineteen stanzas, "Master, how shall I bless Thy Name?" It was used at the International Women's Conference in New York.

She also wrote, "Increase our Faith" and "Reality". This last was pronounced simply perfect by Mrs. Havergal.

It is amusing to none in a November letter to M.V.G.H. that Miss Havergal rallies her on not approving of a Concordance. She says it was past her, and Moody, to imagine why, and asserts, truly enough, that without it it is impossible to know if you have seen every text on any subject.

In the same letter she says she is doing to select 365 texts, and that it won't be done without some spiritual and mental profit to herself. And so closes this year of sickness.

M.V.G.H. says it is not possible to name all the dear Leamington friends who were so kind to Miss Havergal and her mother during this time.

And so F. R. H. came back to the stream of life again. The quiet backwater of twelve months "under His shadow" gives place to movement, and the "silent, suffering year" is over, leaving sweet fruits nevertheless, for "I sat down under His shadow with great delight, and His fruit was sweet to my taste."

Thou art coming, O my Saviour,
Thou art coming, O my King,
In Thy beauty all-resplendent,
In Thy glory all-transcendent;
Well may we rejoice and sing.
Coming! In the opening east
Herald brightness slowly swells;
Coming! O my glorious Priest,
Hear we not Thy golden bells?

Thou art coming, Thou art coming;
We shall meet Thee on Thy way,
We shall see Thee, we shall know Thee,
We shall bless Thee, we shall show Thee
All our hearts could never say.
What an anthem that will be,
Ringing out our love to Thee,
Pouring out our rapture sweet,
At Thine own all-glorious feet!

O the joy to see The reigning,
Thee, my own beloved Lord!
Every tongue Thy Name confessing,
Worship, honour, glory, blessing,
Brought to Thee with glad accord -
Thee, my Master and my Friend,
Vindicated and enthroned,
Unto earth's remotest end
Glorified, adored and owned!

CHAPTER TWELVE
In the Right Place

Miss Havergal seemed in better health in the early part of this year (1876). She heard from India that "Morning Bells" and "Little Pillows" were going to be translated into Hindustani, and that Mission Schools were already using them.

Also the Irish Church Mission funds had not suffered though her illness, for her helpers had rallied round and she felt that they would manage to exceed their previous £50 record.

On one of her visits to friends, she was detained at their house longer than she meant to stay, by a bad cold, and at the same time two lads of thirteen and fourteen were *hors de combat*. Of course Miss Havergal soon discovered where they stood spiritually. They had both been wishing secretly to know that they were safe. So on Sunday, when they pretty well had the place to themselves, the boys came and talked to her. The result of all their colds was that the dear boys came out on the Lord's side, eagerly and certainly.

Still she bemoans the fact that others are doing so much, and she so little. But she is training the choir of St. Paul's, Leamington, and teaching them that they should *so* sing that people may believe - which of course meant that before they could so sing they must be His of Whom they sang. The organist was told that she prayed for his fingers to speak for Jesus.

The choir training was a rare opportunity for evangelistic work. Later we hear of her being choir mistress. It is not clear whether this is at the Thursday services only. But that services was just what she liked best - strongly evangelical and yet "so cheery". "Songs of Grace and Glory" was the hymn book used, and "Havergal's Psalmody," so she would be very much at home at the organ. She was at this time reconstructing the appendix to the former book.

The story of this reconstruction is one of the many "turned lessons" which M.V.G.H. says her sister had - and a very severe one. She had already spent long months on it previously and when the day came on which it was posted ready for press, she had gleefully informed her sister that now she was free to write a book!

A week passed, then came a letter from Messrs.. Henderson's to tell her that their premises had been completely burned down about 4 o'clock that morning. They feared that all the stereotypes of her music were destroyed, for they were in process of printing when the fire broke out. The debris would take many days to cool sufficiently for it to be discovered whether or not any remained. And later news informed her that the musical editions and all the paper had been consumed.

So it was, that instead of writing a book, all the spring of 1876 was occupied in the composition of new tunes - the revision of those sent by other composers, had to be worked out again. Every chord of all the tunes had to be re-examined and as she had not kept one memorandum her own tunes would have to be re-written from memory. All her previous labours were lost, with the exception of a few of the plates which were at the foundry.

A "Turned Lesson," she called (see "The Turned Lesson," Miscellaneous Poems. Nisbet). She accused herself of having hurried the work in order to write her book - work of her own choosing. And now she rejoices in the chance of discovering whether her desire for His will to be done in her is real, or only fancied, and she is resolved to take this reverse as an opportunity of making it "willing service."

Miss Havergal touches the spot here. It is very easy to fancy that we possess certain desires. God, in His tender love. Often proves us to ourselves by sending some trial or test. If the desire is real, we humbly and lovingly submit to His "turned lessons," letting Him work in us that which is well-pleasing in His sight; but is not without a struggle, and not without His help, even though the desire is real. When it is not, we just walk off, and pay no attention to the lesson or the Teacher - so, late on, in His love, sterner measures may have to be used.

Is it not better to take up the lesson and try again? he will help. And again, she says the testing time may show that the lesson is not learnt quite "by heart". She has a deep meaning in those words. We often speak of learning a thing "by heart" and we just man committing a thing to memory. Some people have memorised numbers of texts, verses and hymns but they do not live them. It is surely the honest endeavour to live them which is "learning by heart."

This was not the first time that Miss Havergal had been prevented from plunging into literary work. In 1860 she had thought the door wide open, and that she had only to bound in. But she was, as she expressed it, "kept waiting in the shade." When she was in Switzerland in 1873, she had an object lesson about the shade. It was when she was passing some enormous blocks of ice on the shady side; she noticed how beautifully the sun touched them into colour, and made them iridescent and glittering. Had she been on the sunny side she would not have seen this lovely sight; but she was in the shade, and saw beauties which only that side could show.

Just so with her life - and the lives of many - the world is all the richer because they have been "in the shade".

There is a charming little poem among her "Chords for Children" called "Coming into the Shade" which illustrates this truth - the little one taken out of the sunshine into the shady room because she could not see the pictures in the sunshine. And Miss Havergal, in her facile verses, describes how God's children are brought into the shade so that He can show them what they could not learn in the sunshine.

During may of this year she discusses in letters to M.V.G.H. the question of whether she should leave Leamington and Mrs. Havergal, and live with Marie. There were awkward things at the Leamington home. Miss Havergal had not the freedom she felt she would like, but as she was convinced that she was placed there, she also was convinced that it would not do to leave without perfectly clear guidance.

There was also the likelihood that her health would prevent her being Marie's outdoor helper, unless F.R.H. gave up all her own work. And, she says, the door would be thrown open if it were the Lord's wish, but there must be no forced human opening.

She emphasises the fact that she does not wish to cross her mother in anything, and she is resolved to do what her King appoints.

In another letter she tells Marie of things which have happened to convince her that she is in the right place. God, she says, has shown her that she is of some use there - and so she feels her present path the right one. The instances she gives are remarkable coming at this time. The Rector, the Secretary of the Y.W.C.A., three choir members, the curate, all had a great deal to say, separately, and unknown to each other, as to her helpfulness; and none of them knew of the question in her mind at the time.

The Rector in particular, was assuring. She was obliged to tell him, when he was speaking of choir practices, having agreed to do something he wanted "if she came back in the autumn." That "if" startled him, and of course she could not but explain.

Then he became very earnest, though he did not wish to stand out against what was right, and told his very astonished listener that she had an exceedingly important sphere there. That there would be grief and great loss if she left St. Paul's. F.R.H. gave Marie permission to write freely to Mrs. Havergal if she felt inclined. If the mother was against it - well - where F.R.H. was, was the right place.

There does not seem to be any further reference in the letters to this, and we know that Miss Frances Ridley Havergal did not leave the Leamington home during her mother's lifetime.

Dear Blind Sister

Dear blind sister over the sea
An English heart goest forth to thee.
We are linked by a cable of faith and song,
Flashing bright sympathy swift along;
One in the East and one in the West
Singing for Him whom our souls love best,
"Singing for Jesus," telling His love
All the way to our home above,
Where the severing sea, with its restless tide,
Never shall hinder and never divide.
Sister! what shall our meeting be,
When our hearts shall sing, and our eyes shall see!

~ In 1872, Frances Ridley Havergal paid this tribute to
Fanny Crosby, her sister hymnwriter in America.

CHAPTER THIRTEEN

Marie and Frances in Switzerland

The turned lesson - reconstruction of "Songs of Grace and Glory" Appendix - meant that it was very difficult for Miss Havergal to arrange a holiday, for it was necessary to be where a piano was handy. The proofs of the music were coming to her during the summer, and it was doubtful at first whether she would be able to finish the corrections by August, so that she could accompany her sister Marie to Switzerland.

As the weeks went by, F. R. H. stuck to her work bravely, and was rewarded by bringing it to a successful conclusion in record time.

On 6th July, the sisters set off. They left for Dieppe, and so the Lausanne. M.V.G.H. enjoyed this, as she well deserved to do. Miss Frances Ridley Havergal took care that Marie should see with her all the lovely places she herself had revelled in, and Marie, in her letters speaks of her sister's unselfishness in visiting all the old spots in order to give her pleasure.

Now and again Marie succeeding in persuading her to go off alone. One visit was from Montreux to see Miss E. J. Whately at "Les Avants" - a friend to whom so many of Miss Havergal's letters are written.

Then they went from Vernayaz to Fins Hauts. One Sunday, seeing peasants passing their door early on the way to mass, naturally gave the thought of a Bible address for them.

How could it be managed, they queried, F. R. H. singing snatches of hymns meantime in her clear voice. Then the door (literally and metaphorically) was opened. The good hostess and her father appeared, to request more singing. F. R. H. seized the opportunity of asking about the meeting, and the pair agreed that if Mademoiselle would sing to them all, they would produce an audience for her. Splendid!

But of course the audience must sing part of the time too, so F.R.H. set about writing some french verses *"Seulement pour Toi,"* founded on "Only for Thee" and some others. They came quite easily to her.

The time for the meeting was three o'clock, but before that time several girls arrived and were promptly set down to copying *"Seulement pour Toi"* - the words of which they would never forget. She emphasised in this hymn Christ only as having done all, and as being all - against the Romish "Mary and Jesus".

About forty people come. There was a room beyond the folding doors of the one the sisters occupied, and many sat there. Among these was the priest's servant, who instigated talking and laughing, hoping to disturb the meeting.

Miss Havergal sang to the assembly first, then prevailed on the girls to sing the hymn they had copied. Then she read some verses from Romans and was followed by M.V.G.H. who spoke on Romans 6:23: "For the wages of sin is death, but the gift of God is eternal life through Jesus Christ our Lord." After the brief address she closed with prayer.

Of course there was a sort of undercurrent of opposition. Some of the people indeed left as soon as F. R. H. began to read the Scriptures. But a good number remained and listened.

When the meeting was over, and the people gone, M.V.G.H. remarked that the hymn must be shown to M. Le Cure, who had been in her thoughts all week. "But how will you send it?" inquired the astonished Miss Frances Ridley Havergal. "Take it myself, to be sure!"

F.R.H. thought she was only joking, but suggested that it might be possible to ask him if the verses were correct according to French poetry rules.

"Very well. It's a good excuse for calling on him. And I shall also ask him to lend me a French Bible."

So she went. The priest received her pleasantly, loaned her a Bible which had Romish annotations, and as for the hymn, he looked through it and inquired was the writer French? - a question which seemed to prove that it was all right. And then Marie took the opportunity of telling him of the peace and joy which was to be found here and now in the Saviour and in Him alone. The priest seemed quite interested, and was most courteous; and M.V.G.H. on her part, felt relieved at having spoken to him. Doubtless she was Spirit-led, and one must feel that M. Le Cure was intended to receive that message.

Miss Havergal says Marie was full of delight over their Swiss tour. She was pleased with every place she was taken to. Her sister found this condition of mind "so very nice" and says Marie was delightful to travel with, for their ways did so fit. Also, like F.R.H. she had a great and fine appreciation of the beauties around.

In this long and interesting letter, which is written from Argentieres, on July 24th (to their mother), F. R. H. describes the journey from Lausanne, July 13th; a lovely sunset and beautiful sail to Montreux up the lake. It was from Montreux Miss Havergal went to see Miss Whateley. She went by mule.

Marie, meanwhile, went farther on, to Chillon - its walls close down to the water's edge - where "the fishes swam close to the walls." Did Marie think of Bonnivard, the prisoner of Chillon, who had watched his brothers die there, and he stood, "a slave among the slaves," gazing on the last of the beloved ones? Bonnivard, who when they set him free, says:

> I felt as they were come
> To tear me from a second home.
> It was the same to me -
> Fettered or fetterless to be.

and, he "regained his freedom with a sigh". Poor Bonnivard!

Looking up at the Deut du Midi against the blue sky, Marie would be more likely to muse on Him Who has set us free for Eternity.

The sisters met again in the train for Vernayaz, and there, whilst F. R.H., as courier, engaged rooms for the night and mules for next day, Marie went to see the Gorge du Trient.

July 15th found them at Fins Hauts, where they stayed nine days, instead of three, as they originally intended. Here she interpolates the information that they paid 4 francs per day, and no extras.

They had a glorious picnic here one day. Starting at 6 a.m., they climbed slowly and easily the mountain paths till they reached a spot from which they could see Mont Blanc. But, unfortunately, after a time, the flies drove them to another place, where they consoled themselves with a picnic tea. M.V.G.H. made a fireplace with stones, and built up a splendid fire of fir cones. And there the sisters stayed till sunset, after which they set off homewards, reaching their lodgings just in time to prevent their anxious landlady sending her husband to look for them!

July 24th, they walked down Argentieres, arriving in the sunshine at ten a.m., just in time to escape a terrific thunderstorm. Their rooms here were bright and lofty, and on a separate landing. Mont Blanc could be seen from the windows, and "any amount of Aiguilles" - and they could view sunsets without the necessity of even leaving their rooms - had they so desired.

On to Orsiere by diligence, with the passengers signing French songs. The sisters, as soon as opportunity offered, beguiled them into singing a new tune, and "*Seulement pour Toi,*" which went well.

They spent Sunday at St. Bernard's Hospice. There were crowds of peasants there sitting about on the rocks as they partook the Hospice hospitality, and the two sisters were briskly sowing the Gospel seed here and there.

In the saloon Miss F. H. Havergal sang to the guests by request of the "father" after dinner. The message which she sang, first repeating it in German and Italian, and stating that it was from the Holy Scriptures - was Handel's "Comfort ye," then "He shall feed His flock," concluding with "O Rest in the Lord."

From the Hospice they went on to Martingny and Champery. At the latter place they found Mr. & Mrs. Rogers of St. Paul's Leamington. Mr. Rogers was taking duty as summer chaplain at Champery.

Here, at their Pension, Miss Havergal made the acquaintance of the Baroness Helga von Cramm. The two started a series of Alpine Cards, which later were published by Cassell & Co. The Baroness painted them and F. R. H. wrote the verses.

From Champery to the Bernese Oberland next and a long stay at the Pension Wengen, Lauterbrunnen, with Murren in view. But Miss Frances R. Havergal got drenched in a thunderstorm, and fell ill. They had to stay on at the Pension a month, eventually having it all to themselves. The weather was beautiful for them.

October came and nearly passed, whilst she gathered strength for the homeward journey. They had not anticipated so long a stay, but faith and peace were triumphant. Everything was right. She said she could not look up into her Lord's face and tell Him she did not trust Him in all things.

And so this first visit to Switzerland together came to an end.

It is pleasant to see how very happy and enjoyable it was to the sisters, despite Miss Havergal's long illness. Indeed, we may be sure that even during the illness and convalescence there were many precious days which would linger in the memory for a long time. Happy times in the sunshine and the clear bright air - and just "we two".

CHAPTER FOURTEEN
Everyday Things

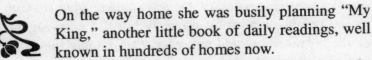 On the way home she was busily planning "My King," another little book of daily readings, well known in hundreds of homes now.

One of her poems "The Thought of God" was published in the Sunday Magazine at this time (1876). She considered it "the very best" she had written but naively remarked that she had not heard that it had done real good to anyone. She thought that the things mostly used were poems which had seemed to her scarcely worth writing out! That much loved, much sung hymn, "I Gave My Life for Thee" (written in 1858) she did not even intend to keep, but threw it into the fire. It did not burn; it just tumbled out again, so she smoothed it, and put it away. Some time after she read the verses to her father and he liked them entirely. His tune "Baca" was written for them.

With all her high spiritual ideals, we might be led to think that Miss Havergal was not practical. But, she was eminently so. And all spiritually minded men and women ought to be practical. There is something lopsided if they are not. We all need what someone has aptly termed "sanctified commonsense".

"A mind to blend with outward life, whilst keeping at Thy side," perfectly expresses it.

Miss Havergal had some very decided views on "dress" and on "giving".

As regards the former. A Christian woman is a "King's daughter". "The King's daughter is all glorious within," therefore, as far as she is able she must dress like a King's daughter, not to be a "fright" outwardly. We have seen many such among very good woman who could easily afford to be prettily and suitably dressed. F.R.H. said she felt she ought to dress "as a lady and a Christian". But she would never spend more than necessary; the rest could be given to God's work. The body must be properly but not extravagantly, clothed. And she would never wear unsuitable things. For instance, she could wear without apology at home a dress which it would be quite slighting to wear at a dinner or a party. She would visit the Infirmary in a different attire from that which she would wear on festive occasions. Her chief aim was "dressing unremarkable" on every occasion, and by so doing avoid attracting attention.

Her views are suitable for all. And the above rule could be carried out by any Christian girl, if she will exercise "sanctified commonsense."

On "giving" she is equally practical. She does not advocate putting all we have into the first collecting plate, but spending that sum which we have set apart for God's work as thoughtfully and carefully as we spend on ourselves. She says that once she intended to give away every penny she earned to the Lord, but when she was stricken down with fever she realised that doctors and nurses must be paid, and that it was not right of her to give all away. She must have a reserve for illnesses. It was not just to expect her relatives to pay her bills. And thenceforward she used her "sanctified commonsense" in this matter.

In another way she was able to gratify her desire for giving by disposing of all her ornaments, including the handsome cabinet in which she had kept them. By this transaction she realised £50 and had no hesitation in giving it to the C.M.S.

This method has, I am glad to say, been used by hundreds, and goodly sums given to the Lord's work. One sees it often in George Muller's biography - which reminds me that my readers will find his life story and example the best lessons on giving that can be had. In the Yearly Reports on the work he started there are entries of many in our present day who sell valuables, or send them to be sold for the good of the work. No more anxiety then about valuable rings, brooches and necklaces.

But it is not right to give to the Lord's work if you are allowing yourself to drift along without paying what you owe to man. "Owe no man anything," and we have no right to give away that which belongs to anyone else, surely.

There is one thing of value we should possess - the ornament of a meek and quiet spirit, which his of great price. It cannot be sold, and need not be stolen!

1877 was a quiet year for Miss Havergal. She did not go abroad for the dear mother's health was giving them all much anxiety.

In June, F.R.H. was at Mildmay. She caught a cold at the Association Meeting, and falling really ill with it, was adequately nursed by Mrs. Pennefather, a very determined lady, who thought nothing of bundling her visitor off to bed and keeping her there.

During the visit she was taken to Clapton House by Mrs. Pennefather. She was so pleased with the place that she said she would like every girl she cared for to be in such a lovely Christian school. The girls knew who F.R.H. was before she visited the school, and she found that they used her little books. When the Principal asked her to take the Bible Class, she readily and joyfully promised to do so. There was a good gathering. She had a dozen in the drawing room afterwards, for special questions, and they clustered "niece-fashion" all around her, as they talked.

Of course they did not expect to see her there again, but in consequence of her detention at Mildmay Park by the cold, she visited them once more and spoke with them in the drawing room.

At one of the Mildmay meetings the speaker announced that Miss Frances Ridley Havergal was present and they hoped for a few words from her. F. R. H. thus rudely awakened from the snugness of her supposed incog. position, remained still and silent. "She *is* here," was repeated, and there was nothing for it but for F.R.H. to rise and say something. She said she was there to learn only!

At this same meeting Mrs. Hudson Taylor was present also Mrs. Emma Boyd Bayley the author of "Ragged Homes and How To Mend Them" and many other people of repute. No wonder F.R.H. felt more like learning.

In September, her niece Miriam died, six days after the birth of her baby. The young people had been married in July of 1872, only about five years. F.R.H. stood sponsor for the little boy - but she herself in less than two years' time was where Miriam had gone. She speaks of a tiny cousin, Maud Prestage, who had also reached the Home above about this time.

Writing to the author of "Never Say Die" (N.S.D. for short) she mentions two more of her books - "Royal Commandments" and "Royal Bounty" - which she had managed to write. But she had been obliged to refuse to write several articles, for her mother had insisted on her being quiet for a bit, and not taking up any outside work.

Also there is a letter to Miss Elizabeth Clay, who is in India (1877), with best wishes for her first birthday there. And thus, in spite of its quietness, the year had brought its changes.

1. Who is on the Lord's side?
   Who will serve the King?
   Who will be His helpers
   Other lives to bring?
   Who will leave the world's side?
   Who will face the foe?
   Who is on the Lord's side?
   Who for Him will go?
   By Thy call of mercy,
   By Thy grace divine,
   We are on the Lord's side,
   Saviour, we are Thine.

2. Not for weight of glory,
   Not for crown or palm,
   Enter we the army,
   Raise the warrior-psalm,
   But for love that claimeth
   Lives for whom He died
   He whom Jesus nameth
   Must be on His side.
   By Thy love constraining,
   By Thy grace divine,
   We are on the Lord's side,
   Saviour, we are Thine.

3. Fierce may be the conflict,
   Strong may be the foe,
   But the King's own army
   None can overthrow.
   Round His standard ranging,
   Victory is secure,
   For His truth unchanging
   Makes the triumph sure.
   Joyfully enlisting,
   By Thy grace divine,
   We are on the Lord's side,
   Saviour, we are Thine.

4. Chosen to be soldiers
   In an alien land,
   Chosen, called and faithful,
   For our Captain's band,
   In the service royal
   Let us not grow cold;
   Let us be right loyal,
   Noble, true and bold.
   Master, Thou wilt keep us,
   By Thy grace divine,
   Always on the Lord's side,
   Saviour, always Thine.

CHAPTER FIFTEEN
The Mother Passes

The winter of 1877 and the spring of 1878 were months of great suffering for Mrs. Havergal.

Again and again in the letters of her mother, F.R.H. comments sympathetically on the constant pain she was suffering long prior to this. Nevertheless, ailing though she was and frail, the brave woman continued to superintend her meetings, Zenana, and A.F.W. Society, as long as this was possible. She was always a most intense worker - had been a wise and loving counsellor to many - a loving and cheery friend to all - as well - as was proved by the response of the Leamington friends in sympathy and help, both for Frances and her mother. One old friend is very specially mentioned - Miss Nott.

In January, Miss Marie V. G. Havergal came to bear a share in the nursing, and F. R. H. was sent to Oakhampton. Whilst there she was busily engaged in writing "The Royal

Invitation". It is a message to the unsaved. A Royal Invitation, we know, it is not allowable to refuse - and F.R.H. in this little book achieved her long-cherished, darling wish - that of levelling her darts at those who are not "the King's children".

The letter in which she speaks of the book is written to G.S.P. (sometimes S.G.P) and it seems that it must be the artist, Sydney G. Prout or his son. He was the author of "Never Say Die," the little book which F.R.H. so admired, and which she was largely instrumental in launching. In this letter, written from Oakhampton, she speaks of a photograph near the piano which she was in the habit of gazing at whilst she sang - a photo of a picture, and she asked her sister Miriam about it only a few minutes before writing to "G.S.P." Miriam said it was a photo of a picture of St. Ouen, by S. G. Prout, "your friend", an answer which pleased and surprised F.R.H. so much that she starts a letter to him forthwith.

In another letter, Feb. 14th, 1878, she says that "The Royal Invitation" is absolutely finished. Next she wants to revise "The Ministry of Song" and "Under the Surface" with the idea of making them into one volume, and leaving out pieces which she considered poor.

Then there is to be a further book of poems, "Daily Melodies for the King's Minstrels". And so her busy mind and fertile brain planned this and that, so much of which she was not able to accomplish for, though they knew it not, her days were running out.

One can see from her letters to her beloved Marie, who is nursing the suffering mother, that she feels her place is at home. Marie is to say when F.R.H. should return, and will Marie please order "The Spanish Brothers" by Deborah Alcok, for a birthday present. It was rather a favourite book with F.R.H. I may say that I have never read a story which makes the Lord Jesus Christ so real, so precious, and in times of torture and death so all-sufficient.

In another letter she gives an instance of the kindness of a publisher Mr. Parlane. Mrs. Duncan Mathieson, widow of the well-known hymnwriter, owed Mr. Parlane £30. The account reached her the day after her husband's death, and when Mr. Parlane received the amount from her he promptly returned the money, thus giving immediate proof that what God has promised He is able to perform (see Phil. 4:19). F.R.H. who knew the publisher and the widow, was grateful and pleased.

The weeks pass by, and she is at home again with Marie and the dying mother. Every day Mrs. Havergal was growing slowly worse. Professional nursing had been necessary now for some time and Nurse Carveley was evidently a great comfort. But even with that help poor Marie broke down once after hours of incessant watching. Miss Havergal was very anxious about that, remembering, however, with trembling hope the gracious words, "I have prayed for thee that thy faith fail not." And her faith did stand this great test: she came through triumphantly and Marie revived.

On Sunday, May 26th, they watched beside the poor unconscious one all night, expecting every moment that she would pass without regaining consciousness. But at last the eyes opened and she recognised Frances kneeling beside her. The first smile they had seen for weeks overspread the drawn face - a smile of surpassing sweetness for the faithful daughter And then the worn spirit passed into the presence of the Lord where there is no more pain. She was buried in Astley Churchyard.

The following months were full of work in one way and another. The breaking up of the Leamington home, of course, was the heaviest consideration.

Before then they went to The Mumbles, where they were joined by their brother. It was a quiet and restful time. After that came a spell in Herefordshire - "Highlands" a farm near to Titley. Close by is the yew tree under which Miss Havergal wrote her poem "Zenith".

There was tent work among other things at Bewdley, and Miss Havergal's nephews and nieces were very enthusiastic.

Marie was in Switzerland and was very ill most of the time, as a result of the long strain of nursing in the previous May.

Miss F. R. Havergal spent part of this summer with Mr. Henry Havergal's widow and family in Somerset. Then she paid a visit to Devonshire. And then the sisters made their home at The Mumbles, where they previously had such a peaceful time recruiting after the dear mother had gone. Five months after that sad event, they were settled in their Welsh home.

Miss Frances R. Havergal had a study after her own heart. There is a minute description of it in "Memorials". I can at least give a few details.

It had two windows, one south, one west. From the south window there was a view of Ilfracombe, from its west window Caswell Bay; and from this window the two sisters would often watch the sunset.

Among her pictures was "The Martyrs in Prison." These were Bradford, Cranmer, Latimer and Ridley. As her own middle name was Ridley, and bestowed on her by a descendant of the martyred Bishop, this picture was greatly valued by her.

In this room, amid her treasures, and with congenial surroundings, Miss Havergal settled down, October 1878, to her usual busy life. The correspondence she received each morning was very heavy. People seemed to think she was a General Encyclopaedia, and had nothing to do but answer letters, revise poems by request of author, and so on, *ad lib*.

And all the time musical proofs are arriving, which had to be promptly and carefully attended to.

She was ill on her last Christmas morning, but there was much writing to be done, for the inspiration which came to her was overflowing.

Marie speaks of her New Year Greeting, January 1st, 1879: "He crowneth the year with His goodness," and then Frances says that one of her mercies is Marie. One can see how sweet this was to Miss Maria V. G. Havergal.

In "Memorials" there is given a "list of mercies" for three months, written in a tiny journal, the gift of Mrs. Charles Bullock, and it is a list of singular significance. So may we:

Count our many blessings,
Name them one by one,
And it will surprise us
What the Lord hath done!

She lived in the spirit of her hymns and
touched the world with her words.

CHAPTER SIXTEEN

You Are Going Now

She went to London at the end of January. Writing from Blackheath, she asks MVGH for a poem of her father's, for Mr. Bullock's book on the Royal Family. Then she announces that she had been photographed. It was done by Messrs Elliott & Fry, who were both present. Mr Elliott himself fetched her. There were eight exposures. She says later that she was feeling chilly and out of sorts when taken, and when the photos arrived expressed the opinion that they did not give her the idea of a lady, and she had always fondly imagined herself to be one!

However, there are many like Miss Havergal, whose charms cannot be reproduced by photography. I had a dear friend like that. She had a radiant, beautiful face, as one saw her. "Such a glow about her," someone said. Only a few months before her sudden Home-call, I picked up a photo from her mantelpiece and asked, "Who is this?" *"Me,"* laughed she, and as I compared that glowing face with the photo I quite excused myself for not recognising it. Miss Havergal's "glow" and vivacity would not photograph. She declared she would never go through the ordeal again.

During this visit to London she made the acquaintance of her publishers - Mr Robertson, Mr Watson (who had been ill), and Mr Hutchings, and tells Marie in her letter that it might be a good thing, for future years, to be personally known to them.

She met Mr Eugene Stock, too, and was delighted with him.

Then comes a rather startling letter (February, 17th) from Charing Cross Hotel, to Marie. Mr and Mrs Bullock have sent her away at a moment's notice almost, as there was a case of smallpox, and they felt anxious to have her out of harm's way. The doctor said the home must be cleared of visitors immediately. So she went straight to a small room at the Hotel, and spent the day, Sunday, by a fire. No fear of infection, but simply the rational course - and then, on Monday, she left for The Mumbles, by the express.

Marie was at Winterdyne, but Miss Havergal, in spite of that, simply rejoiced to come *home*.

Glorious sunshine, and a stack of letters in her study. One can picture how she would revel in it all, sitting by her fire in peace and quiet, knowing that the dear sister would soon rejoin her.

She speaks of "a spree" she had - getting Temperance Pledges from every one in the house (February 21). Also she sends loving messages to her sister Ellen (she is writing to Marie), and assures Ellen she has found Phil. 4:19: "My God shall supply all your needs according to His riches in glory by Christ Jesus," always stands!

She mentions, too, that she has spent £100 to help with someone's premium - and will hope to do more next year. Well, "she being dead yet speaketh".

And she declares she finds it great fun to earn money to give away. Her spirits are very high, and very good at The Mumbles - the home of her last seven months of earthly life. Looking at it from a human standpoint, one cannot but wish she might have lived a little longer in the enjoyment of it. It seems like "song that ceased ere scarce begun," and we must wait for the day in which we shall see the reason for these seemingly regrettable happenings.

In a letter to the Irish Church Mission Collectors she speaks of a little plan she intended to carry out, but was hindered in it, so she'll try it "next year." And "next June" she was expecting to go to Ireland herself.

The Collectors' Text for the current year was: "Be not weary in well-doing." We are weary soon. For instance, now that the newness of the work was gone, is not there rather inclined to be one feeling? How apt we are to take a thing up with great enthusiasm, and then, after a while, to wish we *could* - if we do not actually - lay it down. Not so must the Collectors for the Irish Church Mission behave.

There is some very tender and wise advice in a letter to a girl who thinks someone is in love with her. The danger is pointed out of dwelling too much on attentions, which after all may mean nothing. If they are too greatly cherished, and magnified, what grief there will be if they should not come to anything more. The thing to do was to go and tell out all before the Saviour, and seek His help and guidance, and or strength to endure, if need for endurance arose. Miss Havergal shows her young friend that she has been through it all - some years before. Also, she has had to give a very decided refusal, not long ago, to another proposal. Her great wish and prayer is that the girl may not be in doubt.

She had an interesting interview with Mr Ira D Sankey, in May of this year, a few weeks before she passed away. He was alone in England at this time, and not in very good health. More than once he had been obliged to retire from his post at Mr Moody's side on that account, and very sorely did Moody miss him. But at this time Mr Moody was in Northfield, Massachusetts, beginning the erection of his Seminary for girls who lived too far away in the hills for education, and good Scripture study. Indeed, he was actually then altering his own house to receive the students. The Seminary was opened in November 1879. Mr Sankey would then be more at his colleague's side. Meantime, in England, he is trying the song "Loving all along;" with Miss Frances Ridley Havergal, with the idea that he should sing it in America. At first he did not take to it, but told her later that it struck, and he would do it.

The Baroness von Cramm liked the song, too, and Miss Havergal wrote to SGP (author) that if those two, in their respective circles, would sing it, it would mean infinitely more than any ordinary person singing. It was brought out with her tune by Messrs Hutchings and Romer.

She speaks again of her projected visit to Ireland on Irish Church Mission work on June 4th (D.V.). She intended to take Willie or Alfred Shaw with her round the Irish stations. The work was growing very large, and the time was coming for full organisation of it. Mr Bullock, in his magazine, *Days of Days,* left two pages for the use of Irish Church Missions. But Miss Havergal, before 4th June by just a few hours, had reached the Land of far-stretching distances towards which she so often turned her longing eyes during her busy life.

Her Temperance work, "Newton Temperance Regiment" as she called it - for her boys predominated, progressed splendidly.

She was also re-writing her little book "Kept", and beginning a book for invalids, "Starlight Through the Shadows" and "Morning Stars," all of which were finished before May 9th, and published after her death. She was proof-correcting on May 26th.

But all this writing did not prevent the gathering in of Temperance Pledges at the same time. All the children between eight and eighteen, except four, had sighed. Nor was this all, for, more than anything she desired to win souls for Christ. She visited wherever she could at the cottages, and frequently at the village school, where she won the deepest love. She encouraged the children to learn the Scriptures by offering a new Bible to every child who could perfectly repeat the fifty-third chapter of Isaiah.

Miss Elizabeth Clay was with the sisters at Easter. The Baroness Helga von Cramm was with them in May. They had some pleasant seashore strolls, and when the Baroness was sketching the Lighthouse, Miss FR Havergal was sitting at her side.

The Baroness was of the opinion that FRH looked in good health, and she was certainly very busy with her writing, and her letters, and her Gospel Temperance work, almost to this last week of her earthly life.

On May 21st she was having a meeting on the village bank, but clouds and cold wind came up as it does in this lovely but treacherous month. When she got home she was chilled to the bone.

The next day was Ascension Day, and she went to the Communion Service. Being very tired, she rode a donkey on the return journey, with quite a retinue of her lads. Very solemnly she spoke to one and another. Marie heard from this one and that one later on, the last words her dear sister had spoken to them.

In the evening Miss FR Havergal visited a young sailor lad in his home. He was sailing the next morning. This visit was the last she ever paid, for on May 23rd she was much worse. Not going to those evening Temperance Meetings, so Marie went, taking with her one hundred and fifty Temperance Cards to be given away. During her absence Miss Havergal was very busily occupied making strong paper envelopes for sailors to keep their leaflets in. But she had to give up, and Mary, the faithful maid, who had so often escorted her to meetings, and packed and unpacked, and generally tended her, had to help her to her bedroom.

She was very feverish next morning, and, of course, unable to set her friend, Baroness Helga von Cramm, forward on her journey. The Baroness left, not anxious about Miss Havergal, as these feverish attacks were of frequent occurrence. That anything serious was the matter she never guessed, nor that her next meeting with her loved friend would be in the presence of the Lord.

The day was full of spiritual thought and spiritual converse for Miss Havergal. She asked Marie to arrange her wall-texts in a special way. And there was a little picture by the Baroness - a glacier -and the words: "I saw a sea of glass, clear as crystal," on it, which lifted her thoughts heavenwards.

She did her proof correcting on the 26th. The next two days she was feebler, and she asked the doctor if she was likely to go, but he did not consider her at that time so very ill. It would seem that her brightness and happiness made it difficult to gauge her state exactly. She he thought "not yet."

But on May 29th inflammation set in, and peritonitis. Nurse Carveley who had nursed Mrs Havergal, was with them. The sisters and the brother Frank came down. She was anxious to cheer them all, and told them that her pain and sickness simply meant that she would be Home the sooner. Indeed, she affirmed that "it seemed too good to be true," that she was going.

On Whit Monday they feared she was passing, but the feeble flame flickered up once more. She continued to tell them how near the Gates she was, and how lovely it would be to go through them.

She asked her brother Frank to sing, "Jerusalem, my happy Home" to their father's tune "St Chrysostom," and with the verse: "Jesus my Saviour dwells therein." Next they had "How sweet the Name of Jesus sounds."

Mr Morgan, the Vicar of Swansea, who called to see her asked if the Saviour was with her now. Her reply was most emphatically given - *He is!* By Mr Morgan she sent friendly messages to many she knew.

Mrs Morgan called that afternoon, and to her Miss Havergal repeated the age-old assertion: "Not one thing hath failed of all the good things which the Lord your God spake concerning you; are all come to pass unto you, and not one thing hath failed thereof" (Josh. 23:14).

Later on her brother Frank sang "Christ for me, Christ for me," and how true for her:

When my life draws to its close,
Safe in His arms I shall repose.

Her sister Ellen repeated:

On Christ the Solid Rock I stand,
All other ground is sinking sand.

Once she asked if she would be disappointed of going, and they assured her that they were certain that she would soon reach her Heavenly Home. To quote an old book: "You are going now," said they, "to the Paradise of God." And again: "There was a post come from the Celestial City, with matters of great importance ... So the post presented her with a letter, the contents whereof were: 'Hail, good woman, I bring thee good tidings, that the Master calleth for thee.'" That letter brought, not fear, but an unspeakable joy to Christiana. FRH had no fear - she sang that wonderful hymn "Jesus, *I do* trust Thee."

Then came a rush of sickness, and Nurse Carverly, after helping her, laid her gently down on the pillow.

Frances folded her hands on her breast, and sighed with relief, and for ten minutes they watched her radiant face. Once more she tried to sing, but after one clear note, her breath failed - but, "Behold, all the banks beyond the river were full of horses and chariots, which were come down from above to accompany her to the City Gate." Beyond that gate she was in the Presence of her beloved Saviour.

The frail body was laid to rest in Astley Churchyard - in sight of the room in which she was born. Over the tomb spread the branches of the fir tree which her father had planted. Sometimes the sun would shine through those branches on to the quiet spot; sometimes inclement snow and rain would fall upon it. But she recks not of that. Her bright spirit is rejoicing in Heaven, with its "splendour, shadowless and broad."